Self-regulation in education is a familiar and important topic for all educators: professors, administrators, teachers, researchers, journalists, and scholars. As educational standards require that students take control of what and how they learn, self-regulation skills are essential to student success. Written by a leading expert on self-regulation and self-regulated learning, this book situates the topic within the broader context of educational psychology research and theory, bringing it to a wider audience. With chapters on the fundamentals of self-regulation, explanations of its uses, and advice for best application, this concise volume is designed for any education course that includes self-regulation in the curriculum. It will be indispensable for education researchers and both pre- and in-service teachers alike.

Jeffrey A. Greene is Associate Professor in the Learning Sciences and Psychological Studies program in the School of Education at the University of North Carolina at Chapel Hill, USA.

Ed Psych Insights

Series Editor: Patricia A. Alexander

JEFFREY A. GREENE

Self-Regulation in Education

Routledge
Taylor & Francis Group

NEW YORK AND LONDON

First published 2018
by Routledge
711 Third Avenue, New York, NY 10017

and by Routledge
2 Park Square, Milton Park, Abingdon, Oxon, OX14 4RN

Routledge is an imprint of the Taylor & Francis Group, an informa business

Library of Congress Cataloging-in-Publication Data
A catalog record for this book has been requested

ISBN: 978-1-138-68909-1 (hbk)
ISBN: 978-1-138-68910-7 (pbk)
ISBN: 978-1-315-53745-0 (ebk)

Typeset in Joanna MT
by Apex CoVantage, LLC

Contents

Acknowledgments

This text was a delightful challenge, and I am grateful to Patricia Alexander and Dan Schwartz for the opportunity to tackle it, and for their ongoing support throughout the process. Further, I owe much to Barbara Greene and Daniel Dinsmore, who were invaluable sources of feedback and encouragement. The anonymous reviewers for this text provided very insightful critiques as well. Dale Schunk has been a wonderful collaborator and mentor, and his insights on self-regulated learning have been tremendously helpful. Finally, as always, I am profoundly grateful for my family, Mira Brancu, Avery Greene, and Jacob Greene.

One

Why Study Self-Regulation in Education?

In an era of rapid technological advancement and extraordinary feats of human ingenuity, why do students continue to struggle to obtain more than a rudimentary understanding of the topics they learn in school?[1,2] Why has the Internet's proliferation of information sources and democratization of information distribution had little to no discernable effect upon the quality of human decision making?[3] And why do employers continue to lament today's workers' inability to exert initiative and problem solve?[4] The answers to each of these questions are no doubt complex, but the questions themselves highlight an important point: deep conceptual understanding, nuanced critical thinking skills, and the ability to make positive contributions in the work world involve knowledge and skills that are not innate, intuitive, or easy to acquire.[5] Thankfully, such knowledge and skill can be learned, with effort and guidance.

Stories of entrepreneurs, leaders, and humanitarians illustrate common learned lessons, skills, and beliefs that underlie their success. These individuals set clear, valued goals in which they invest significant personal motivation. They make plans for how to reach those goals, even if sometimes those plans must be made as they rush forward. Throughout pursuit of their goal, they maintain belief in themselves, their goal, and their capacity to attain it. They persist in the face of obstacles, both of others' and of their own making, and when necessary they choose the more difficult, less intuitive, but more availing path. They understand and shape their emotions to fuel positive outcomes and beliefs. They seek out feedback, from themselves and others, to chart their progress and change course when needed. Finally, they engage in productive dialogue with themselves and the people around them, being responsive to their world while also working to change it for the better. Often the individuals chosen for these stories seem to be outliers in terms of their actions, their circumstances, or both. Nonetheless, the actions, skills, and beliefs necessary to succeed in the modern world are not unusual or unattainable. They can be learned, and they are the focus of this book: self-regulation in education.

The academic literature on self-regulation in education tends to fall into two camps, each of which addresses issues of critical importance to education and learning in the twenty-first century. In one camp, including but not limited to education, educational psychology, and learning sciences researchers, are those who study self-regulated learning (SRL), often defined as "the processes whereby learners personally activate and sustain cognitions, affects, and behaviors that are systematically oriented toward the attainment of personal goals" (p. 1).[6] Self-regulated learners have both the "skill" and the "will" to learn. They possess skills to learn, such as effective learning strategies, and they know which of those strategies work for them in learning situations. They also have the will to learn, including positive motivation to get them started on a learning task and the volition to help them persist through to completing the task, even when it gets difficult. These skills and wills are powered by positive emotions, as well as positive interpretations of their emotions, whether they are positive or negative ones. Self-regulated learners actively manage themselves, their thoughts, and their surroundings, including the other people in those surroundings, to maximize their learning efforts.

SRL is needed for a wide variety of academic tasks, such as learning how to solve problems, writing accurate and convincing arguments, tackling unfamiliar and open-ended tasks, and engaging in the kinds of inquiry necessary to really understand how science works and how it can inform public policy, among other educational tasks. Numerous studies and reports have endorsed SRL knowledge and skills as powerful predictors of achievement in school and life-long success at work.[7,8,9] Indeed, SRL has begun to be embraced as not just a way to achieved desirable educational outcomes but a valuable educational outcome in and of itself, as evidenced in recent educational policy and standards movements.[10,11,12]

On the other hand, there is a second camp of scholars, often including but not limited to cognitive, developmental, and social psychologists, who study self-regulation in multiple contexts, including but not limited to formal and informal educational environments. For these scholars, self-regulation involves how people actively monitor, adjust, and maintain levels of cognitive, motivational, and emotional arousal in ways that fuel, rather than derail, their pursuit of goals, particularly in the face of challenges.[13,14] From this perspective, self-regulation pervades all aspects of human functioning, such as when people pursue challenging goals such as losing weight, saving for retirement, or interacting in positive ways with teachers and peers in school. Even after controlling for prior achievement, IQ, and other internal and external factors, students' self-regulatory processing predicts health, marital harmony, financial success, criminal activity, and, yes, a variety of academic factors including performance, school readiness, and relations with other students and teachers in schools.[13,15,16] The unique predictive validity of self-regulation is unsurprising when considering how often during the course of a school day students must recognize when their initial response is not getting them what they want, and instead must replace that initial response with a more effortful yet more effective one, such as when students who are teased inhibit their impulse to lash out, and instead respond more positively, such as seeking help from a teacher or school counselor.

Given the valuable contributions of both the SRL and self-regulation literatures toward understanding school readiness and success, both areas of scholarship must be included in any comprehensive introduction to self-regulation in education. The SRL literature provides detailed, actionable models of how people approach specific learning tasks and contexts, and how they can do so more effectively.[17] These models are descriptions of the components of SRL, how those components interact with and influence one another, and the different roles those components play as people begin a learning task, work to complete a learning task, and then reflect upon their performance once the task is done.

The self-regulation literature also provides models of the development of individual differences in self-regulatory functioning, within and beyond academic tasks, as well as how those differences relate to not just learning itself but also all of the other important events and interactions that occur in education contexts, such as making friends, navigating complex rules, and managing the emotions that arise in classrooms, hallways, and lunch rooms over the course of a school day. To discuss either SRL or self-regulation research without the other would be to paint a useful, but nonetheless incomplete, picture of how students self-regulate in education contexts.[18] Parents, educators, researchers, and of course students themselves would benefit from focusing on developing students' capacity for both SRL and self-regulation.

BRIDGING THE TWO LITERATURES

Why do these two camps, SRL and self-regulation research, remain largely uninformed of one another? One answer lies in the siloed nature of academic research. SRL research tends to be done by education, educational psychology, and learning sciences researchers, who are most typically found in education departments. The broader study of self-regulation often involves research in non-education contexts, and the scholars who do this work often reside in psychology departments. Unfortunately, despite recent efforts to support collaborative and cross-disciplinary scholarly interactions across university departments, such work is the exception still, and not the rule. There is a critical need for scholars who can break down and traverse these silos to study self-regulation in education, and some researchers have begun this work.[18,19,20] Nonetheless, there remains vast untapped potential in efforts to bridge these two literatures.

Origins of SRL and Self-Regulation Research

A second reason for the siloed nature of these two literatures has to do with their origins. The nature of this text precludes a detailed history of SRL and self-regulation research, and indeed other texts exist for this purpose (e.g., Zimmerman & Schunk, 2003).[21] A brief discussion of the fields' origins is helpful, however, to understand why they have not intersected as much as might be expected, and to understand differences in terminology and focus. The SRL literature began with the application of Bandura's[22] social cognitive theory to issues of learning and education.[6] Bandura's work on how people learn from others (i.e., social cognition) was born in psychology, but, in its application to education, social cognitive theory was merged with ongoing research in education on strategy use, metacognition, and motivation.

In the late 1970s and early 1980s, research on students' strategy use was evolving due to the findings that simply teaching students effective strategies was no guarantee they would actually use them, particularly when confronted with problems outside of the context in which those strategies were taught (i.e., students did not "transfer" learned strategies to new problems or contexts). Findings regarding students' difficulty with transfer informed research on metacognition, or how people think about, and experience, their own thinking, strategies, and the thinking of others.[23] Metacognition research led to insights regarding how to help students understand why certain strategies were better than others, and the conditions under which particular strategies should and should not be used. Metacognition researchers also explored how students monitored and controlled their understanding of both content and the efficacy of various learning strategies.[24] It also led to innovations in how to help students understand and act upon the feelings they experienced during learning, such as confusion.[25] However, researchers found that even effective metacognitive training would not necessarily guarantee that students would apply or transfer the effective learning strategies they knew. Motivation research revealed how students' goals, efficacy, and identity could influence the likelihood of them enacting and transferring cognitive and metacognitive strategies.[26,27] In short, metacognitive and strategy knowledge was not enough; students had to want to use and transfer this knowledge. Modern SRL research was born out of intentional integration of social cognitive theory with learning strategies, metacognition, and motivation research.[37]

Self-regulation research, on the other hand, evolved out of psychological studies of behavior and emotion management. Whereas behaviorists and early scholars of self-management focused on behaviors and emotions as negative things to be shaped and controlled, over time researchers came to understand the importance of also helping people leverage their positive cognition, emotions, and behavior to achieve desired goals.[14] Work on intentional, adaptive management of the self to achieve desired goals spanned the entirety of human functioning, including, but not focusing upon, educational or learning contexts. Connections to education contexts were made, such as in test anxiety and school readiness research, but much of that work has focused upon helping students overcome impediments to learning (e.g., test anxiety, poor relations with peers and teachers), rather than how to successfully complete particular learning tasks in literacy, mathematics, or science, for example.[15]

An overly simplistic but helpful heuristic is that much of the SRL research has involved studying how students can effectively pursue academic goals, whereas self-regulation researchers have focused on how students can best manage their well-being so that they can focus on academic goals. The siloed nature of SRL and self-regulation research is unfortunate given that students do not live their lives with clear separations between academic tasks and the non-academic aspects of formal and informal education environments. Over the course of the school day, students must enact both SRL for academic goals and self-regulation for non-academic but educationally relevant goals.[38] Students must study effectively for their math tests while also finding time to make and sustain friendships. Trips to the science museum involve both learning something about biology or physics and learning how to talk about evolution in a productive way with a relative who endorses creationism. In short, students must balance their academic and well-being goals,[36] and they benefit from support and instruction on how to enact both SRL and self-regulation effectively.

Shared Capacity for SRL and Self-Regulation

The literatures on SRL and self-regulation must be bridged for another important reason. Students who struggle self-regulating their learning often struggle to self-regulate their interactions with peers and adults in education.[13,38] Likewise, students who must frequently enact self-regulation to deal with a myriad of challenges in school (e.g., overcoming fear of failure, managing feelings when seeing peers with more resources than they have) or at home (e.g., poverty, family strife) often have fewer resources, and often less interest, in learning and invoking SRL for academic tasks.[39] Prominent models of self-regulation account for these effects by describing how people have a limited amount of resources to engage in self-regulation.[35,40] Self-regulation, whether it be for academic (i.e., SRL) or broader well-being goals, is effortful; therefore, enacting it requires spending some of this limited amount of resources. These resources can be replenished only after a period of rest. Therefore, when students' resources are depleted, they are less likely to enact successful self-regulation in education.

Until recently, this shared resources view of SRL and self-regulation has received little attention, particularly in education research.[18,20,36] Conceptualizing SRL and self-regulation as drawing from the same limited set of resources leads to a number of insights. First, the shared resource model of SRL and self-regulation provides another plausible explanation for why some students do not enact or transfer effective learning strategies: sometimes they know what to do, and are motivated to do so, but lack the necessary resources to exert the effort to enact or transfer due to other stresses in their life. Second, it is important for students to learn and master adaptive SRL and self-regulation strategies, beliefs, and motivations, because once mastered these strategies, beliefs, and motivations require less resources to enact, leaving more resources for other challenges.[13,14] Students who have mastered effective strategies have more resources available for the day-to-day self-regulatory challenges that can arise, such as trouble at home, or conflicts with peers or significant others. A third insight is that the shared, finite resources used for SRL and self-regulation means whenever possible, students should be miserly with these resources. SRL is a powerful predictor of academic performance, but that does not mean that students should consciously and effortfully enact planning, monitoring, control, and evaluation for every learning task; such work would exhaust students by lunch time. Rather, effective SRL means enacting it only when needed; students who have mastered particular learning tasks likely should not enact conscious SRL because it is not needed. Students who are adept at regulating their emotions likely do not need to spend a lot of time reflecting upon them over the course of a school day. Indeed, there is evidence that asking students to slow down and consciously enact previously mastered skills can lead to poorer performance.[41] One final, perhaps obvious, insight is that helping students learn and enact effective self-regulation in education, the focus of this text, requires understanding both the SRL and the self-regulation literatures.

TERMINOLOGY IN SELF-REGULATION IN EDUCATION

Like many academic literatures, the terminology in SRL and self-regulation scholarship can be confusing. The terminology within disciplines can vary greatly, with different researchers using the same terms for different ideas. For example, there has been a great deal of debate regarding the proper definition of the terms "self-regulation," "self-regulated learning," and "metacognition."[42] Some researchers have defined the term "self-regulation" very narrowly, including only the control of emotions, whereas other researchers have defined the term "self-regulation" quite broadly, meaning all the cognitive, metacognitive, motivational, volitional, and emotional processes involved when people pursue goals in the face of personal, interpersonal, and situational challenges.[13,14] Other scholars have argued that self-regulation refers only to control processes and should therefore be conceptualized as one process among many (e.g., planning, monitoring) enacted during metacognition. On the other hand, scholars have debated whether the term "metacognition," with its focus solely on cognition as opposed to motivation or emotion, should be conceptualized as one aspect of self-regulation.[42]

Given this variability in terminology, when writing texts covering SRL, self-regulation, and metacognition, there is great temptation to simply ignore the differences in terminology entirely and simply call everything "self-regulation" or "self-regulated learning." However, doing so puts readers at a disadvantage when they encounter varying terminology in other sources within and among the literatures. Therefore, in this text, attention will be paid to various terms in the literature, and how they do and do not overlap. The additional complexity this approach adds is warranted given how the understanding of this complexity prepares readers for moving beyond this text.

To avoid contributing to the terminological complexity in the fields of SRL and self-regulation, only the most modest of a new terminological hierarchy is needed (see Figure 1.1). In this text, the term "self-regulated learning" (SRL) refers to all aspects of self-regulation in the pursuit of academic or learning goals, and it encompasses the literature in education, educational psychology, and learning sciences research. SRL can occur in formal learning environments such as K–12 schools and higher education, as well as in informal learning environments such as a museum or at home when studying.

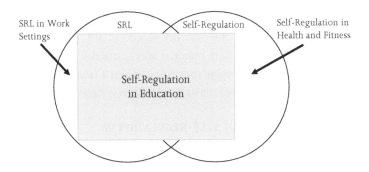

Figure 1.1 Relations Among Self-Regulation in Education, Self-Regulated Learning, and Self-Regulation Terms and Literatures

The term "self-regulation" refers to pursuit of well-being goals, both personal (e.g., losing weight, buying a house) and social (e.g., having positive relations with other people). The focus of this text will be self-regulation that happens in formal and informal learning contexts, such as when students inhibit their automatic response to yell at a teacher because of a bad grade and instead ask for additional help, or when students self-reward themselves for spending a sunny Saturday in the library studying.[36] The overarching term "self-regulation in education" refers to the SRL and self-regulation that students do in formal and informal educational environments.

As shown in the figure, there is some research on SRL that is not conducted in learning or education settings (e.g., the study of SRL in work settings),[43] and quite a lot of research on self-regulation outside of education settings (e.g., dieting); these literatures are indicated by the parts of the two circles that fall outside of the gray box. In addition, there are aspects of self-regulation in education that are beyond the scope of this text (e.g., socially shared regulation),[44,45] but they will be discussed briefly and connected to the foci of this text in Chapter 5.

Finally, in this conceptualization of self-regulation in education, metacognition is one of many aspects of SRL (e.g., when a student predicts whether material was learned well enough to pass a test) and self-regulation (e.g., when a student anticipates how others will react to a particular response).

ASSUMPTIONS ABOUT SELF-REGULATION IN EDUCATION

The terms "SRL" and "self-regulation" often invoke two assumptions that need to be debunked. First, some people assume that self-regulation is an innate quality that cannot be changed or altered; this an understandable but incorrect assumption. According to dynamic systems theory,[46] even the most fundamental aspects of self-regulation in education, such as attention or inhibitory control (see Chapter 2 for more on these processes), evolve through a multi-determined, interactive process between nurture and nature. In short, individual differences at birth are not the sole or primary predictors of later functioning, nor are environmental factors. Rather, these two broad categories of factors, along with the decisions autonomous humans make, interact over the course of human development, resulting in dynamic patterns of development and performance. Students' self-regulation in education performance at any particular time is the result of these dynamic interactions, but thankfully genetic differences in self-regulatory capacity (i.e., nature) play a smaller role in actual self-regulation than what students experience and learn about how to self-regulate (i.e., nurture).[47] In short, all students can learn to more effectively and autonomously self-regulate in education.

The second common assumption about self-regulation or self-regulated learning is that the onus of responsibility for regulation falls solely upon the student, or the "self." Again, this is a reasonable but incorrect assumption. Models of self-regulation and SRL quite appropriately place a great deal of weight upon how external factors can influence self-regulatory functioning, although these models do so to varying degrees and in somewhat different manners.[48] For example, even the most knowledgeable and adept self-regulator will struggle in extremely hostile or challenging environments, and likewise those who consistently struggle to self-regulate can be successful in particular contexts, with particular supports. Helping students to be more effective at self-regulating does not absolve educators, and society in general, of the responsibility to create environments where the need for self-regulation in education, particularly in response to negative events, is invoked as infrequently as possible. Likewise, efforts at bolstering students' self-regulatory skills are a necessary complement to, but not a substitute for, society's efforts to address structural inequalities. Indeed, there is growing evidence that the negative effects of structural inequalities, such as poverty, social inequality, and structural racism, extend well beyond opportunity and achievement gaps and into the likelihood of students enacting effective self-regulation.[15] Therefore, students' success at self-regulation in education certainly depends upon the students themselves, but external factors play a critical role.

One example of how multiple innate, personal, and contextual factors interact to determine functioning involves a common self-regulatory process: delay of gratification. People's likelihood of being able to delay gratification, when they choose to do so, is due in part to biological differences in terms of reactivity to stimuli, but also due to qualities of the environments they experience over the course of their lives (e.g., did they grow up in environments where needs were met and resources abundant, or in environments where others were neglectful, with scarce resources?), as well as various personal factors (e.g., has the person learned strategies to make delaying gratification easier, and what kinds of attributions for success and failure to delay gratification has the person made in the past?) and the immediate context (e.g., is peer pressure present, and what are the consequences of failing to delay gratification?). Even if knowing and controlling all of these factors were possible, which they are not, the best that could be done would be to estimate the *likelihood* that this person would delay gratification; it is not possible to say with 100 percent certainty whether a particular person, in a particular context, will successfully self-regulate in education.

Thus, self-regulation in education is not something that students either can or cannot do, nor is it something that is totally dependent upon individual or contextual influences. In many ways, this is a hopeful view of self-regulation, because it allows every student to aspire toward better self-regulatory knowledge and skills and because it promises rewards for those who engage in the hard work of developing such knowledge and skills. Likewise, educators and other influential members of educational contexts can focus their energies on creating environments where successful self-regulation is more likely, but perhaps less needed, for all students, rather than spending energy in the misguided pursuit of determining who can and cannot self-regulate. In sum, a positive, growth-oriented perspective, quite different from many common assumptions about self-regulation in education, informs this text: individual and contextual factors can increase or decrease the likelihood self-regulation occurring, but these factors are malleable and subject to change over time.

SCOPE OF THIS BOOK

In this opening chapter, the broad parameters of this text have been outlined. Self-regulation in education includes both the literature on SRL and the literature on self-regulation.

These literatures connect and inform one another, although much more work is needed to fully explore and strengthen these connections. This text is an attempt to further that work. In addition, self-regulation in education is defined as malleable and learnable rather than static and innate. Finally, self-regulation in education does not mean that students should be held solely responsible for navigating their learning or education. True, students who have effective self-regulation knowledge, skills, and beliefs are more likely to succeed across varied contexts, compared to their peers who, for whatever reason, struggle to self-regulate. Nonetheless, society should create educational systems and contexts with the goal of fostering effective learning, and one way to do that is by teaching and supporting self-regulation in education.[47]

The second chapter in this book contains the bulk of the conceptual literature review necessary to understand the current scholarship on models of self-regulation in education. This includes an integrated conceptualization of SRL that synthesizes the commonalities among many models of SRL, and it serves as the working model for this book. A review of self-regulation research from cognitive, developmental, and social psychology fleshes out the conceptualization of self-regulation in education and shows how self-regulation and SRL research can be helpfully connected. This chapter ends with a discussion of how SRL and self-regulation develop.

There are vast literatures on how SRL and self-regulation relate to various academic processes and outcomes, which will be reviewed in Chapter 3. Various syntheses of this literature, including conceptual and meta-analyses, will be used to identify the current state of the art in self-regulation in education research, as well as promising directions for future research. There is increasing interest in how SRL might be enacted differently across academic disciplines or domains (e.g., history, science, mathematics, learning with computers)[49,50,51] and this chapter ends with discussions of SRL research from each context.

In Chapter 4 the growing literature on educational interventions for self-regulation in education will be reviewed. This literature spans a number of different types of interventions, with a myriad of targets including achievement within and beyond the classroom. Again, a full review of the entire literature is beyond the scope of this book, but a synthesis of findings will reveal current evidence on the qualities of productive interventions, as well as a sense of what future research is needed to understand how to teach and support self-regulation in education even more effectively.

Finally, Chapter 5 recapitulates the main points of the other four chapters. This summary informs a discussion of future directions for research and practice related to self-regulation in education. Despite having an already large volume of research informing it, there is still much to be done to better understand and foster self-regulation in education.

Two

What Is Self-Regulation in Education?

Having traced the broad outlines of research on self-regulation in educational settings, it is time to explore the phenomenon in depth. This chapter begins with models of SRL. The SRL literature boasts a strong conceptual core.[52] Since the introduction of the term of SRL,[37,53] many researchers have posited their own model, each of which varies less in terms of the phases (e.g., before, during, and after learning) or processes included (e.g., task definition, cognitive evaluations), but rather more in the prominence of the various aspects of functioning that can be regulated (e.g., cognition, motivation, emotion). In this chapter, rather than review every model of SRL that has been advanced, the focus will be upon how the various models can be cohered into a common conceptual framework for SRL. However, that is not to say that conceptual work on SRL has ended, or should do so. There is still much to be gained from exploring new ideas about SRL and testing whether they help to describe and intervene upon the processes of self-regulation in education.

Self-regulation research, like SRL research, boasts a strong conceptual core, but one that is also plagued by models with differing terminologies and groupings of functions.[14] Most researchers agree self-regulation ability derives from core, fundamental cognitive processes, often called executive functions.[13] People enact executive functions, including working memory, inhibitory control, and cognitive flexibility, when they pursue goals, particularly when they need to pay attention to what they are doing to achieve those goals. Likewise, executive functions are used when people realize that the typical way they achieve a particular goal will not work, and they must effortfully enact a different strategy or plan. The term "executive" is used to indicate that people use these functions when they consciously and intentionally pursue a goal.

With maturation and experience, these executive functions come to work together to support higher-order cognitive and metacognitive processing, including self-regulation. Debates about which aspects of executive functioning develop first, and what to call them, distract from the more important message: individual differences in executive functioning are predictors of self-regulation, school readiness, and academic achievement. Thankfully, students can improve their self-regulatory functioning with effort and guidance.[15] Understanding self-regulation in education requires familiarity with models of both SRL and self-regulation, including the role of executive functions.

This chapter ends with a review of literature on how self-regulation in education, including both SRL and self-regulation, develops over time and experience. Developmental models of self-regulation in education span both the typical progression of self-regulatory functioning over the course of maturation and how that process is affected by external forces such as education and feedback. These models form the conceptual foundations of effective methods of intervening on the development of self-regulation in education, the subject of Chapter 4.

MODELS OF SELF-REGULATED LEARNING

Implicit Aspects of Models of Self-Regulated Learning

Connecting SRL to self-regulation research requires highlighting things that are often implicit, but not explicit, in models of SRL. For example, many models of SRL focus upon what happens or should happen when students need to self-regulate their learning, such as when first attempting a new learning task (e.g., writing a persuasive essay). Such actions include defining the task, setting goals, enacting plans and strategies, and then monitoring and adapting those plans and strategies when necessary. However, once a learning task has been mastered, or what some call "automated," there is often little need for many of these actions (e.g., planning) when that task must be performed again. This is the first, often implicit, aspect of SRL models: they are better at describing how students approach novel or effortful tasks rather than automated ones.

Indeed, performance can be degraded when students are asked to consciously enact learning processes for tasks that have been automated.[54,55] Imagine asking someone to plan, enact, monitor, control, and reflect upon every step of making a grilled cheese sandwich; it can be done (e.g., "Okay, I guess the first thing I need to do is find the bread, which is most likely on the counter, so I will start my search there . . ."), but it will take much longer than simply letting that person make the sandwich as he or she has in the past. Therefore, any discussion of SRL must come with the caveat that, for many automated learning tasks, students have little need for many aspects of SRL.

Unfortunately, many students fail to recognize when their automated actions are not working, or will not work, for a particular learning task.[5] This is a second, often implicit, aspect of SRL models that must be highlighted: sometimes students do not realize that SRL is needed. SRL models do an excellent job of describing how to thoughtfully engage in tasks, but many students struggle to determine when such thought is and is not necessary. Students often encounter such difficulties when transitioning between schooling contexts. Often, the motivations, cognition, and behaviors associated with success in elementary school are less effective in middle school. Many students struggle with the increased autonomy of middle school, such as the expectations that students make their own way from class to class, and that they track homework themselves with few reminders from teachers.[56] Often, newly minted middle school students have to experience a few setbacks before realizing that the automated strategies that worked so well in elementary school (e.g., depending upon reminders from teachers) must be amended in middle school.

The third often implicit aspect of SRL models is that students often have to actively manage the simultaneous pursuit of multiple goals, some of which are academic, and others which are more personal or social (i.e., self-regulation). Given the limited resources available for self-regulation,[35] sometimes students choose to regulate in ways that take them further from their academic goals but closer to their personal or well-being goals. For example, when a first-year college student gets a poor grade on a persuasive essay assignment, there are many potential explanations for this outcome. It could be due to internal factors (e.g., a failure to understand the task, the implementation of inappropriate strategies), external factors (e.g., a lack of prior education in effective writing, a professor who dislikes the student), or a combination of both. Reflecting upon the process of completing a learning task, and diagnosing the reasons why it was or was not successful, are themselves often challenging, non-intuitive processes that unfortunately few students have automated. The emotions and threats to self-concept that often arise from such reflection can lead to students abandoning their academic goals (e.g., getting a good grade on the essay assignment) in lieu of what they perceive to be more important personal, non-academic goals (e.g., maintaining their self-concept of themselves as a "smart person"). Some models of SRL explicitly acknowledge these non-academic goals and the balancing students must enact between them and academic goals (e.g., Boaekerts),[36]) whereas others do so only implicitly (e.g., Zimmerman).[17]

Finally, there is a fourth, often implicit, aspect of SRL models. For a model of SRL to be complete, it must describe both successful and unsuccessful self-regulation and generate reasonable hypotheses of why some students enact SRL well whereas others do not, and why SRL is more likely in certain contexts compared to others. One of the major goals of SRL research has been to understand why students fail to self-regulate effectively at times, so educators can help students learn to do so. Much of the early research on SRL focused upon comparing expert and novice students' processing and behaviors before, during, and after learning, to determine what differentiated the successful students from those who struggled.[37] This research led to valuable prescriptive models of SRL: in essence, they described what students *should do* when they need to self-regulate their learning. However, numerous researchers have pointed out that there is also value in a descriptive approach to modeling SRL, which involves observing and describing all of the things students *actually do* when they should be self-regulating while learning, whether what they do is effective or not.[24,36] Indeed, there are instances when students (a) do not notice discrepancies between their performance and their desired goal (e.g., failure to focus sufficient attention on the learning task), (b) fail to self-regulate when they know they should (e.g., procrastination), (c) self-regulate toward suboptimal or even damaging goals (e.g., making excuses to protect their ego rather than admitting and correcting an error), or (d) enact maladaptive or less-efficient processes because they have faulty beliefs about cognition, strategies, or other aspects of learning (e.g., believing smart people do not have to work hard to learn).[5] Models of SRL are most helpful for researchers, educators, and students when they describe ways students self-regulate both successfully and unsuccessfully, and how they can increase the likelihood of the former and decrease the likelihood of the latter. In sum, combining models of SRL requires attending to both their explicit and their implicit aspects.

Combining Models of Self-Regulated Learning

The model of SRL presented here is an amalgamation of numerous predominant models (i.e., Zimmerman, Winne, Pintrich, Boekaerts, Efklides). A combined model is possible because there is a great deal of overlap in terms of (a) the various aspects of functioning that can be self-regulated (i.e., targets of SRL), (b) the typical order in which people enact SRL (i.e., phases of SRL), and (c) the actual things people do to self-regulate their learning (i.e., processes of SRL). Models of SRL primarily differ in the degree to which certain targets, phases, or processes are emphasized. The goal here is not to provide details of each model and how they do and do not resemble one another; for such a discussion, interested readers can consult a number of primary and secondary sources (e.g., Schunk & Greene,[57] Winne & Hadwin;[58] Zimmerman[17]). Instead, the goals here are to (1) describe SRL, including all of its *targets*, *phases*, and *processes*, (2) discuss how interactions among the various aspects of SRL occur over the course of completing a learning task, and (3) show how the results of such interactions can influence how students pursue a wide variety of potential goals in formal and informal education settings, including academic but also well-being and social goals.[36]

Targets of Self-Regulation

Any aspect of learning that can be consciously contemplated and controlled is a potential target for self-regulation. Most models of SRL address six broad categories of self-regulatory targets: cognition, metacognition, motivation, behavior, affect, and the external environment. Each category contains numerous specific aspects of learning, which can and should be targeted when necessary.

Cognition

Cognition generally refers to thinking focused on the learning task itself, including task definitions, goals, plans, learning strategies, and self-judgments. Despite being a somewhat neglected aspect of student thinking and research, task definitions are important aspects of cognition because they inform students' goals.[59,60] Students are not a tabula rasa.[61] When given an academic assignment or task, students construct their own interpretation of it. Even relatively simple assignments can be open to interpretation. For example, when a teacher says, "Finish the mathematics worksheet," one student might construct a task definition of "Finish the mathematics worksheet as fast as possible," whereas another might construct "Finish the mathematics worksheet with no mistakes." These differing task definitions can influence the kinds of goals students set, the strategies they use to complete the task, and how they judge whether the task was completed successfully or not.

One reason why students struggle in school is because their task definitions, and the goals they set because of them, do not align with those of their teacher. Differing task definitions can explain a poor grade on a persuasive essay assignment, such as when first-year college students incorrectly assume that their high-school teachers' focus on historical facts (i.e., what happened, when it happened, who was there) will be shared by their college history professor, who instead wants students to develop historical inquiry and thinking skills.[62,63] In these cases, the professor and the student had very different definitions of the task itself, which in turn led to very different ideas about what a "good" essay was.

Goals are another critical aspect of cognitive processing during SRL. There is a vast literature on the various kinds of academic goals students set, along with empirical research on how different kinds of goals can lead to very different learning behaviors and outcomes.[64] However, the majority of this literature falls within the domain of motivation theory; therefore, it will be discussed in the section on motivation as a target of self-regulation.

The plans students make to achieve their goals are another target for regulation. Planning quality and level of detail relate to academic outcomes, particularly when learning tasks require more than automatic processing.[59,60] Unfortunately, many students fail to plan at all, or they make relatively crude plans, both of which make it difficult for students to adequately monitor their progress or recognize when a change in strategies is needed. For example, many students make a plan focused upon time spent learning (e.g., "I am going to spend two hours on mathematics, then one hour on literature"), which leads to monitoring their progress based upon inappropriate outcomes (e.g., "Well, it has been two hours so I am done!"). Instead, plans should focus on the efficiency and quality of the work completed (e.g., "I want to write a good paper as quickly as possible").[17]

Given that one of the origins of SRL is research on learning strategies,[17] it is not surprising that much of the conceptual and empirical literature on cognition in SRL focuses on the types of strategies students use, their efficacy, and their efficiency. It is not enough for a student to be aware of a strategy (i.e., declarative knowledge) or how to use it (i.e., procedural knowledge). Students must also possess the conditional knowledge of the circumstances in which particular strategies are, and are not, most helpful.[65] For example, taking notes on a laptop may be necessary when instructors present a large amount of novel information during a lecture but be maladaptive when instructors use lecture time to synthesize and expand upon previously covered material.[66]

There has been a recent uptick in research on effective strategies for learning,[67] but a definitive list of effective strategies remains elusive for good reasons. Despite evidence that there are some strategies (e.g., rereading) that are low-utility regardless of other factors, the utility of most strategies depends on many internal or external factors such as the amount of prior knowledge the student possesses and the desired learning outcome (e.g., recall versus application of information). Nonetheless, studies have shown that experts have a large repertoire of learning strategies; the declarative, procedural, and conditional knowledge to use them effectively; and the ability to monitor their efficacy and adapt them as needed.[17]

Finally, after completing the learning task, potential cognitive targets for SRL include judgments students make about themselves and their work. Self-evaluations are judgments students make about themselves based upon the quality of the work they produced during the learning task (e.g., "I did not do well in calculus, so I must not be a math person"). Students who have inaccurate task definitions, have unclear goals, have poor plans, or use ineffective strategies often end up making inaccurate and maladaptive self-evaluations. Whether the learning product is judged a success or a failure, students make attributions as to what caused that outcome. Attributions can be adaptive (e.g., "I worked hard; that is why I did well") or maladaptive (e.g., "I am stupid; that is why I failed"). These attributions can be classified along three dimensions: whether they are internal or external (i.e., due to the self or due to factors outside of the self), unstable or stable (i.e., likely to change in the future or not), and controllable or uncontrollable.[68] Research has shown that it can be particularly maladaptive to attribute success or failure to internal, stable, uncontrollable factors such as innate ability or genetics.[69] The causal attribution literature connects strongly to various ideas in motivation research, including mindsets research, discussed later.

Metacognition

Metacognition is most commonly defined as "thinking about thinking" or, in other words, mental processing where the target is cognition itself.[23] Modern definitions of metacognition include five subcomponents: metacognitive knowledge, metacognitive skill, metacognitive experiences, goals, and strategies.[70] Metacognitive knowledge includes knowledge of how people learn, both people in general (e.g., "Self-testing is an effective strategy for promoting recall") and how individuals themselves learn (e.g., "I learn better when I study in a quiet place"). Metacognitive knowledge also includes knowledge of tasks (e.g., "Persuasive essays should include an argument, counterargument, and rebuttal") and strategies (i.e., conditional knowledge). On the other hand, when people monitor their learning progress, decide they need to make a change, and then subsequently choose among numerous alternative strategies, they are utilizing metacognitive skills. Metacognitive experiences include a wide variety of judgments and evaluations, such as ease of learning judgments (i.e., how much effort is it taking to achieve this task?), feelings of knowing (i.e., how likely is it that a piece of information is known, even if it cannot be recalled at the moment?), and judgments of learning (i.e., if given a test on the content being learned, what is the likelihood of doing well on that test?).

Definitions of metacognition can be difficult to reconcile with SRL literature for several reasons. First, the definition of metacognitive knowledge of strategies is very similar to the definition of conditional knowledge, which is often considered an aspect of cognition in SRL models. Second, metacognitive skills—including planning, monitoring performance, and evaluating the quality of work produced—seem to overlap substantially with processes described in self-regulation research, in general, and SRL, in particular. Third, goals and strategies were included in the "cognition" target, previously. Here again, the siloed nature of science, in this case education research, can result in confusion for readers familiar with one literature (e.g., SRL research) but not with another (e.g., metacognition research in psychology). Nonetheless, in this combined model of SRL, these confusions can be reconciled. Plans and strategies are things created and used to complete learning tasks; therefore, they belong in the cognitive target.

Metacognitive knowledge is knowledge about cognition; therefore, it is appropriately labeled as a "meta" concept; in other words, conditional knowledge is metacognitive, but declarative and procedural knowledge are cognitive in nature. Metacognitive knowledge can be monitored and controlled; therefore, it is a "target" of SRL and belongs in this section. On the other hand, the "metacognitive skills" aspects of most definitions of metacognition in the psychology literature (i.e., planning, monitoring, controlling, evaluating) are part of the "processes" of SRL, described later. They are not "targets" of SRL; rather, they involve how SRL is enacted. Therefore, in this model, the metacognitive targets of SRL are metacognitive knowledge and experiences, because they can be consciously contemplated and controlled.

Motivation

The education research literature on motivation is vast, including work on learners' goals, interest, beliefs, and dispositions.[27] Within each of those categories of motivation there are a number of different posited constructs and models of how those constructs relate to numerous academic processes and outcomes, including SRL. For example, scholarship regarding one model of academic goals, called achievement goal theory,[71] includes debates about whether there are two, three, or four relevant motivational constructs (e.g., mastery approach, performance avoidance), as well as evidence of varying and somewhat conflicting relations between those goals and desired academic outcomes. Likewise, self-efficacy, or a person's confidence in being able to complete a task successfully, has been shown to be a powerful predictor of academic outcomes,[64] but there are continued debates about whether students have general academic self-efficacy, discipline-specific self-efficacies (e.g., a student's history self-efficacy could be different than a student's mathematics self-efficacy), or even task-specific self-efficacies (e.g., a student could have high self-efficacy for geometry but low self-efficacy for algebra). The enunciation of these debates and the varying empirical findings in the motivation literature is not meant to criticize the field; rather, it is evidence of the vitality and relevance of motivation as an educational phenomenon. What is important for understanding SRL is that motivation is a key predictor of students' choice of task and their likelihood of constructing task definitions, goals, and plans necessary to complete that task.[34] Indeed, Zimmerman[72] has identified self-efficacy as one of the primary predictors of whether students enact SRL at all. In general, motivation provides energy and direction for learning, and it tends to be conceptualized as a key factor in the before phase of SRL.

Motivation can be a target of SRL, and researchers have called this process metamotivation.[26,28,29] There are strong parallels between metamotivation and motivation, and metacognition and cognition. Metamotivation includes knowledge of the various kinds of motivation (e.g., goal orientations, self-efficacy, values), self-knowledge of what affects one's motivation (e.g., "I know I am intrinsically interested in science, but not in history, so I have to self-regulate my motivation in history more than in science"), and knowledge of various motivation strategies (e.g., self-rewarding). Metamotivation research also includes the processes of monitoring and controlling motivation (i.e., self-regulation of motivation), which, just as with metacognitive skills, will be discussed later. The main point here is that motivation is an important predictor of the likelihood and quality of initial engagement in a learning task and that it can and should be self-regulated.

Behavior

Given the cognitive, and social cognitive, revolutions in psychology, it may seem strange to see behavior listed as a target of SRL separate from cognition. Nonetheless, many models make such a distinction, with the term "behavior" encompassing a number of learning phenomena including time management, future time perspective, delay of gratification, and procrastination.[30] There is ample evidence that many students' automatic behavioral responses can be maladaptive (e.g., poor or nonexistent time management, difficulty delaying gratification), therefore requiring self-regulation. Luckily, there is also ample empirical evidence that more adaptive behaviors (e.g., thoughtful time management, planning, and strategies for overcoming procrastination) can be learned and automatized.[31]

There is significant overlap between research on the self-regulation of behavior and research on volition.[32,33] Volition processes are enacted when students encounter resistance in their pursuit of desired goals.[34] When students continue working on an assignment even when it turns out to be much more difficult, and time-consuming, than they planned, these students are enacting volition. Whereas motivation concerns which goals students choose to pursue, volition involves students' capacity for overcoming challenges, both internal and external, to reach those goals. In the language of the phases of SRL, motivation is a "before learning" phenomenon, and volition is a "during learning" phenomenon. Volition can be monitored and adapted; for example, when students notice that they are no longer reading for understanding but rather just letting their eyes glance over the words, they can adapt by enacting a mental contrasting strategy, comparing their current state (i.e., student) to their long-term goal (i.e., successful doctor) and thinking about how what they are reading will help them achieve that goal. Such contrasting can help students refocus on reading for understanding. Students can also enact volitional strategies such as removing distractors and temptations, which makes it easier to persist during learning. In cognitive and developmental psychology, volition research also goes by the name of self-control research, which is covered in more detail later in this chapter.[35,40]

Affect

For much of the history of psychology and education research, affect (i.e., emotions, moods) was seen as something that must be controlled, lest it interfere with, or bias, effective cognition. Effective thinking was seen as rational, or "cold" in nature. A general "warming" trend has occurred in these literatures as researchers have come to understand that affect plays an essential role in all cognitive functioning and that affect can have both positive and negative effects upon thinking and learning. Experiencing very weak emotions (e.g., boredom) or very strong emotions (e.g., panic) can derail learning. Ideally, students experience a middle-ground, optimal level of emotional arousal, which allows them to focus on learning and increase the likelihood of understanding, recall, and application of the material.[73]

Whereas there has been less research on the role of moods (i.e., general, relatively low intensity, longer-lasting kinds of affect) in education, there is a growing body of work on the role of emotions (i.e., more specific, higher intensity, shorter-lasting kinds of affect) in education, and SRL in particular.[74,75] Emotions can be characterized in three ways: by their valence (i.e., whether they are positive or negative), the degree to which they prompt or defuse action (i.e., activating or deactivating), and their focus (i.e., achievement, topic, social relations). Test anxiety, for example, is a negative, activating, achievement emotion that tends to lead to increased maladaptive psychological and physiological activity such as worrying. On the other hand, pride can be a positive activating emotion where feeling good about succeeding after hard work can lead to the desire to pursue additional achievement opportunities, such as when a student struggles through an introductory course but gets a good grade, resulting in pride and the decision to continue on to more advanced work.

The still-growing body of empirical evidence regarding the role of emotions in SRL suggests that in general students are more likely to plan, monitor, control, and evaluate their learning when they experience positive activating emotions (e.g., surprise), and are less likely to do so when they experience negative deactivating emotions (e.g., shame). However, there is a need for much more research on the likely complex interactions among emotions, students' interpretations of their emotions, and other aspects of SRL processing and performance. Nonetheless, emotions can and should be monitored and controlled when necessary, and much of the literature on emotion self-regulation comes from developmental psychology.[76] As in education, in the past developmental psychology researchers conceptualized emotions as solely a negative influence upon performance that needed to be overcome, but modern models of emotion regulation position emotions as essential aspects of goal striving and attainment.[13,14]

External Environment

Finally, often students must monitor and adapt aspects of the external environment such as where they study, who they study with, and what they allow to influence their learning. Moving from a noisy coffee shop to a quieter one is an example of self-regulating the external environment, as is the choice of a study partner who helps the student focus on learning, as opposed to one who tends to distract the student. There is a large literature on help-seeking and how students can effectively determine when help is needed and then implement strategies to obtain the appropriate amounts and kinds of help.[77] For example, some students seek help to get the correct answer only (i.e., executive help-seeking), whereas other students take a more availing approach by seeking help with understanding a concept (i.e., instrumental help-seeking).[78] Students' ability to monitor and control their external environment depends upon the degree of controllability of that environment, of course. Students often cannot control whom they sit next to in middle school or what time their organic chemistry class is offered. Nonetheless, when possible it is more effective to choose an optimal environment for learning from the outset, rather than exerting effort to attempt to monitor and control a suboptimal environment in the moment.[40] Whenever possible, students who prefer quiet places to study should be encouraged to seek them out, rather than attempting to ignore distractions in a noisy study room. Given the many targets of SRL (i.e., cognition, metacognition, motivation, behavior, affect, external environment), and the limits of human cognitive and emotional energy, it seems wise to make decisions that decrease the likelihood of needing to actively monitor and control one or more of those targets before learning begins.

Phases of SRL

Models of SRL would have little utility if they were simply a list of the kinds of things that can and should be planned, enacted, monitored, controlled, and evaluated. Thankfully, there does seem to be a loosely ordered, recursive set of phases of SRL commonly described as before, during, and after learning.[72] These phases group the kinds of things students do, and should do, to self-regulate their learning effectively. The "before" phase commonly includes things such as defining the task, setting goals, and making plans for learning. Motivation also plays a key role in the "before" phase, and students who realize they lack adequate levels of motivation should self-regulate their motivation (i.e., metamotivation) toward an optimum level to provide the energy and direction for learning. The "during" phase involves aspects of SRL involved with actually engaging in the learning, be it reading a chapter, writing a paper, searching the Internet for information, or practicing how to play the piano. Learning strategies, and metacognitive processes regarding assessing progress toward goals, play prominent roles in this phase. Also in this phase, volition is used to maintain learning efforts, particularly when encountering internal and external difficulties. Finally, the "after" phase of SRL involves evaluating both the results of the "during" phase (e.g., a student's understanding of the chapter, the quality of the paper written) and the processes used to attain that result (e.g., effectiveness of plans, strategies). Evaluations of the process and product can lead to changes in a student's self-beliefs, motivation, and other aspects of future instances of SRL. To the degree possible, students should automatize what they do before, during, and after learning, so they focus on the learning task itself. However, effective self-regulators realize when they are not learning as effectively or efficiently as they would like, and they can shift from an automatized to a more conscious, self-regulated mode of learning.

These phases of learning have been described as "loosely ordered" because sometimes students skip one or more phases (i.e., moving right into "during" learning phase without much forethought or "before" processing).[17] Likewise, these phases are recursive because sometimes students realize that they have to return to a previously completed phase, such as when progress toward a goal is slow in the "during" learning phase and the student realizes that a different plan is needed; this can result in recycling back to the "before" phase. Also, instances of SRL are recursive in that what happens over the course of one learning task can influence future learning. For example, when a student works hard on a paper and evaluates it positively, that can lead to higher self-efficacy for future instances of paper writing, resulting in an increase in the likelihood that the student will engage in adaptive SRL processes.[17] Thus, both virtuous and vicious recursive cycles across learning tasks can ensue, where the results of past performances have positive or negative effects upon future SRL processing and performance.

Before Learning

Whether people need to enact SRL while engaging in a learning task depends greatly on their prior knowledge, the task itself, and the context in which the learning takes place. With that caveat in mind, when SRL is needed, there are a number of things that can and should occur before beginning the actual learning task, including creating task representations and definitions, setting goals and planning, and activating motivation. The order in which these things happen can vary across individuals and contexts, as can the emphasis people place on each. Many of the aspects of SRL that occur before learning were reviewed in the targets of SRL section of this chapter, but two deserve additional focus here: goals and mindsets.

Goals

Students do not simply have academic goals; they also have goals regarding their well-being (i.e., protecting their self-worth) as well as social goals (i.e., maintaining valued relationships with peers). Dual-processing models of SRL[36] account for students' need to balance and self-regulate toward multiple goals, in particular academic or mastery goals as well as personal or well-being goals. For instance, when confronted with a difficult learning task, some students welcome the challenge, seeing it as congruent with both their academic and their well-being goals (e.g., "I am a hard worker, and that quality will help me pass this test, and get me one step closer to medical school"). Other students may have academic goals congruent with the challenge (e.g., "I want to pass this test so I get one step closer to medical school"), but likewise fear what the challenge might mean for their identity, should they struggle or even fail to achieve (e.g., "I am a smart person, but if I fail this test maybe that means I am not smart after all"). In this latter instance, the students might decide that protecting their self-image is more important than striving toward the academic goal, resulting in SRL toward their well-being goal and away from their academic goal (e.g., self-handicapping, making causal attributions to factors outside of their control). Acknowledging the multiple goals students attempt to balance in education settings (i.e., academic, well-being, social goals)[79] leads to the realization that self-regulation in education is broader than just self-regulated *learning*. Students have personal and social goals that also require self-regulation, a topic discussed later in this chapter. Further, pursuit of personal and social goals can be influenced by students' mindset regarding ability, learning, and effort.

Mindsets

Extensive research has shown people have mindsets, or what are called implicit theories, about many things, including intelligence.[69] Implicit theories are fundamental assumptions about the degree to which various personal qualities, such as intelligence, are malleable. These theories are "implicit" because people often do not consciously think about them or realize how they are influencing their cognition, affect, or behavior. Likewise, they are "theories" because they are a filter through which people interpret the world, their own capabilities, and the causes of their performance. These implicit theories affect learning, SRL, and self-regulation because they shape how students make sense of their successes and failures, which in turn can affect how they engage in future tasks in education.[80]

Implicit theories of intelligence, or mindsets about intelligence, range from the assumption that intelligence is fixed at birth and unchangeable (i.e., a "fixed" mindset) to the assumption people can grow their intelligence over time through practice and hard work (i.e., a "growth" mindset). These mindsets influence students' goals, beliefs about effort, attributions, and use of learning strategies.[81] Students with a fixed mindset have goals such as looking smart or not looking dumb, whereas students with a growth mindset set goals of increasing what they know and can do. Fixed mindsets lead people to believe that having to exert effort during learning is a sign of a lack of intelligence, a message all-too-often reinforced by the United States' culture of heralding "geniuses" or "experts" while ignoring the hard work they put in to get to that status. Growth mindsets allow people to properly contextualize effort as the key to improving performance, and a sign of strength rather than weakness. When students with a fixed mindset encounter difficulty, they interpret it as a sign that they are "dumb" or have hit the ceiling of their capacity for doing something (e.g., "I'm not a calculus person"). Students with a growth mindset interpret setbacks as indications that they need to work harder or differently, maintaining their "can do" attitude. Finally, fixed mindset students often give up in the face of difficulty, rather than persisting and trying different learning strategies, which are typical of students with a growth mindset.

Thankfully, mindsets themselves are malleable, and students can change from a fixed to a growth mindset via targeted interventions.[81] Such changes often require self-regulation of self-talk, such as when a student's automatic response to challenge (e.g., "I can't do this, I'm dumb") must be monitored and then replaced with a more adaptive one (e.g., "I can't do this yet, but if I keep at it I will figure it out"). Clearly, mindsets are a powerful aspect of motivation, and research has shown that they can have strong effects upon learning, including what goals are set, how they are enacted and monitored, and the emotions that result.[82] As such, students' mindsets predict a number of important learning phenomena, including the likelihood they enact SRL, persistence, and academic performance.[80,83,84]

During Learning

In this phase, the actual work of learning or performance is done. Again, automated tasks often do not require active monitoring and control of things like learning strategies, but most complex tasks benefit from the monitoring and adaptation of the various targets of SRL: cognition, meta-cognition, behavior, affect, and the external environment. Motivation's powerful influence upon goal pursuit and planning in the "before" phase is replaced in the "during" phase by volition, which determines how and to what degree students persist when encountering difficulties such as confusion or distraction.

Learning Strategies

Effective students have a wide variety of high-utility learning strategies they can deploy when monitoring indicates insufficient progress toward desired goals. These can be cognitive strategies (e.g., self-testing), volitional strategies (e.g., self-rewarding when a task is completed), behavioral strategies (e.g., monitoring time spent on a task), affective strategies (e.g., positive self-talk), and environmental regulation strategies (e.g., seeking instrumental help). However, many learners lack such strategies or are just beginning to automate them. For these students, monitoring and adapting learning strategies is quite effortful and, frankly, exhausting. Therefore, when first developing their ability to enact SRL, students should be prepared for feelings of tiredness or frustration due to having to not only learn the material but also learn how to plan, enact, monitor, control, and evaluate their learning. With deliberate practice, SRL functioning becomes more automated, leading to improved performance, but the process can be initially frustrating for students, particularly those who are already struggling to learn material.[85] This is when support from others can be essential.[44]

Likewise, some students have automated maladaptive beliefs, knowledge, or skills that can have negative effects in the "during learning" phase.[5] For example, fixed mindsets lead to a number of maladaptive beliefs about effort, among other things, that can decrease persistence and increase negative affect. Misconceptions about disciplinary knowledge (e.g., the Earth has an elliptical orbit that brings it closer to the sun during summer and farther away from the sun during winter) can lead to cognitive dissonance when encountering correct conceptions (e.g., "Wait, what does the tilt of the Earth have to do with seasons?") and subsequent poor decisions about what to study (e.g., "This does not make any sense so I am going to move on to something else"). As a last example, self-testing using recognition rather than recall strategies can lead to incorrect assessments of progress toward learning and can bring an inappropriately early end to studying. These beliefs, knowledge, and skills can be changed, but doing so requires first the recognition of the need to do so (i.e., monitoring) and then effortful control. Such control can be difficult to invoke and can deplete energy that would otherwise be used for learning content or performance. Teaching students to do this, particularly in school contexts, is much more difficult than simply pointing out the problematic beliefs, knowledge, or skills, and providing an alternative.[86]

Finally, it is important to note that many of the learning processes and strategies discussed in SRL models are phrased in domain-general language (e.g., monitoring learning, taking notes, elaboration). Such processes and strategies may be sufficient for the acquisition of declarative knowledge (e.g., definitions) but insufficient for the acquisition of high-level procedural or conceptual knowledge, which often varies by academic discipline. The need for further research into the domain-specific aspects of SRL is particularly important given that educational policy in the United States is shifting toward a focus upon not just the acquisition of knowledge but also the ability to critically consume and produce knowledge across disciplines (e.g., Common Core Standards, Next Generation Science Standards).[10,11] Critical-thinking, inquiry learning, argumentation, and other high-level cognitive processes often require discipline-specific strategies.[87,88] For example, argumentation in history requires, among other things, the ability to engage historical empathy skills (i.e., the ability to put oneself in the position of a historical figure, in the figure's historical context, to understand that figure's decision-making and situation),[62] which differ greatly from the skills necessary to engage in argumentation in biology.[50,89] Research on the role of discipline-specific SRL processing and strategies is in its early stages, but it is showing promise, as discussed later in this chapter.

Metacognitive Experiences

Students' monitoring of their progress toward goals results in various metacognitive experiences that serve as moment-to-moment influences upon self-regulation.[75] Metacognitive experiences can include feelings of difficulty (i.e., "This is really hard to read"), feelings of knowing (i.e., "I cannot remember the answer to this question right now, but I know I have learned it before"), judgments of understanding (i.e., "I am really following this explanation well"), and judgments of learning (i.e., "I think I will do well on a test of this material"). Such metacognitive experiences can lead students to reflect upon their progress and, if necessary, cue them to regulate their learning. For example, frequent positive judgments of understanding (i.e., "This makes sense") may lead a student to infer that the content of a chapter is easy or already known, and cause the student to stop reading and start another learning task (i.e., enact control). Likewise, frequent feelings of difficulty can lead students to choose a different learning strategy or, in some cases, abandon the learning task altogether due to frustration. The frequency and intensity of these metacognitive experiences are important data for students to monitor and act upon during learning, but whether students do so depends upon many other internal (e.g., working memory capacity available for monitoring) and external (e.g., how much time is left for the task) factors.

Numerous models of SRL include interactions between more stable, trait-like aspects of students that predict processing across learning tasks in a "top-down" manner and more unstable, state-like experiences that can affect processing during a particular task in a "bottom-up" manner.[75] In essence, top-down factors determine how students typically approach learning tasks, but bottom-up factors, like metacognitive experiences, derive from how a particular learning task is progressing, and can sometimes override top-down factors. For example, students' academic self-efficacy is a relatively stable top-down factor that influences choice of task and persistence across many different learning tasks. However, even students with high academic self-efficacy may begin to doubt themselves if they experience frequent feelings of difficulty during a particular task (e.g., reading a challenging chapter), which may lead to them self-regulating their learning during this task in different ways than would be typical for them (i.e., enacting rarely used, resource-intensive but effective strategies; or self-regulating toward well-being goals by attributing the difficulty to an external factor such as a bad chapter author).

Metacognitive experiences are one example of things that can occur during learning and subsequently lead to "bottom-up" regulation. As another example, monitoring that a task is taking longer than expected (i.e., bottom-up SRL phenomenon) may lead students to enact metamotivation to change their academic goal orientation (i.e., top-down

SRL phenomenon) and achieve their goal. This is not always a maladaptive adaptation; indeed, there are times when things students do in the "before learning" phase result in inefficient or ineffective behaviors in the "during learning" phase, and, by recognizing this, effective self-regulators recalibrate in ways that make it more likely that they invoke more appropriate learning and self-regulatory strategies in the moment and in the future (e.g., seeking help, increasing and spacing study time). During learning there are numerous interactions between top-down and bottom-up factors in SRL, with potential implications for performance on the current and future tasks. Effective SRL involves monitoring those interactions and actively and thoughtfully adapting in availing ways.

Volition

Interactions between learning strategies and metacognitive experiences can influence students' volition (i.e., capacity to pursue desired goals when faced with distractions and difficulties).[90] Volition is crucial in terms of maintaining attention and managing effort for academic tasks. Numerous strategies exist to bolster and maintain volition for academic tasks, such as breaking down large tasks into subtasks, self-rewarding and taking breaks when needed, and analyzing the potential causes of inclinations to procrastinate.[91] As with most aspects of SRL, monitoring and controlling volition during learning requires effort until volitional strategies are automatized. Therefore, there is great incentive for students to practice effective volitional strategies (e.g., the Pomodoro technique of working for some period of time, then taking a short break, then beginning work again), because with practice these strategies become automatic, freeing up resources for learning.

Volition research spans both SRL and self-regulation literatures and shares some common ideas. For example, volition is seen as a finite resource that can be depleted. Likewise, there is evidence that students who believe that willpower is an unlimited resource, as opposed to believing it to be a finite resource, are more likely to persist in their studies and procrastinate less, leading to higher grades.[92]

After Learning

Researchers have focused more upon the "before" and "during" phases of SRL, compared to the "after" phase, perhaps because students often neglect this phase as well. Nonetheless, what occurs after learning matters because students' interpretations of their learning products and processes have implications for how they approach future learning tasks. Students with clear, relevant goals are better able to assess the efficacy and efficiency of the learning, compared to students with unclear or no goals, who often rely on others' evaluations of the learning product to judge their success. Careful monitoring and consideration of learning can also lead to more accurate attributions for success and failure[68] because students have data regarding why they performed as they did.

Students' evaluations after learning are important, but so are the inferences and affect associated with those evaluations. Students who experience positive activating emotions (e.g., happiness, pride) are more likely to continue striving for adaptive goals in the future. Students who experience deactivating emotions, particularly negatively valenced ones, are more likely to privilege well-being over academic goals in future learning situations, using procrastination, task avoidance, and self-handicapping, which can lead to learned helplessness.[93] Of course, these self-judgments and self-reactions are not stable;

complex interactions among students' cognition, motivation, and affect can result in a variety of outcomes. Likewise, these self-judgments and self-reactions are targets for SRL.

Finally, it is important to reiterate that SRL is recursive: what happens in one phase of SRL can affect what happens in later phases, and vice versa. For example, a learner reading a history chapter may make a good plan before learning (e.g., "I am going to take detailed notes on the historical figures in this chapter") only to discover that during learning the plan is taking too long or not covering the most important material. Self-regulated learners will use this information from the "during learning" phase to go back to the "before learning" phase and construct a new plan (e.g., "I am going to take notes on only the major historical figures in the chapter, and make a timeline of the major events as well"). This is an example of recursion within a single learning task.

In addition, SRL is recursive in that evaluations, inferences, and affect that occur "after learning" for one task can influence what a student does "before learning" in the next task. For example, self-regulated learners evaluate the efficacy and efficiency of their strategies in the "after learning" phase, and then use this information the next time they invoke SRL "before learning." Students who realize that verbatim notes are an inefficient and ineffective way to learn new information will, hopefully, choose a different strategy when planning how to complete their future learning tasks. The mechanics of how students monitor and control these self-evaluations, choices of strategies, and other aspects of learning have been denoted and explored from information-processing theories of SRL.[58]

Processes of SRL

An enunciation of what can be targeted when students enact SRL, and a rough order of when different kinds of SRL processing happens, would not really be a model; it is also necessary to describe the processes of SRL: how people plan, enact, monitor, control, and evaluate their learning. To begin, a now-familiar caution must be stated once more: ideally, people do not enact SRL when they have automatized effective plans, strategies, etc. to complete a task, because active, conscious SRL requires effort and working memory capacity that, in most cases, would be better used for completing the task. Students writing the same kind of paper they have successfully written in the past likely have an efficient plan for the work and can assume it will continue to work well for them; in cases like this one, there is no perceived need for them to actively enact SRL, such as constructing a plan in the "before learning" phase, etc. Likewise, students may have a repertoire of learning strategies that, in the past, have worked well for a particular task; therefore, they may not need to spend mental energy choosing among strategies during learning. When students experience positive, activating emotions during learning, there is little need to monitor or control them. Students who automatically make availing causal attributions for success and failure likely do not need to monitor their attributions or replace them with a different one.[68] The point here is that SRL is not necessary when an automatic response is the most efficient and effective way to pursue those goals. Regardless, students may realize the need to invoke SRL processes at particular points over the course of learning (i.e., before, during, or after learning), and not others; indeed, this is effective self-regulation.

Monitoring and Control

That said, the processes of SRL can be described fairly simply, belying their importance in SRL. Information-processing models of cognition, and SRL, have been used to describe these processes, with the two main components being monitoring and control.[24] Students can monitor the adequacy of any of the targets of SRL (i.e., their use of learning strategies, their motivation) as well as the adequacy of the learning product they are producing (i.e., their understanding of a chapter, a paper for a class, their ability to play a sonata on the piano). To do this, students need standards, or criteria, that are used as benchmarks for performance. Standards can be few or many, but it is likely they increase in number and sophistication with experience and the innate complexity of the learning task. Novice learners are more likely to have a limited number of standards because they do not know enough about what adequate performance looks like. For example, novice learners may have limited standards for task definitions (i.e., "Write a paper about Abraham Lincoln"), their own motivation (i.e., "Do better than everyone else in my class"), and the work product (i.e., "The paper needs to be five pages long"). More-experienced learners likely have multifaceted standards (i.e., "My teacher wants a persuasive argument paper about Abraham Lincoln's influence upon modern ideas of freedom. I am not intrinsically interested in Lincoln, but I understand historical knowledge is necessary if I want to become a lawyer, so I am going to do my best to learn and write about Lincoln. I know my teacher expects the paper to have a clear argument, four pieces of primary source evidence for that argument, and a conclusion connecting my argument to current political events. The paper must have no more than two typographical or grammatical errors or I will not get a good grade").

As these products are created and refined in each phase of SRL, students engage in monitoring, evaluating the fit of the product to their standard for that product. When the fit is insufficient, such as when the product meets some but not all of the students' standards, the students must decide whether to continue working on the product or not and, if so, whether they should continue using the same strategies or enact control to adapt. Enacting changes, called control, can include adaptation of the targets of SRL, the standards for the product, or the previous products created over the course of learning (i.e., task definitions, plans). Sometimes students need to adapt the strategies they use (e.g., "Rereading is not helping me to understand; I had better start taking notes"), whereas other times they need to adapt standards (e.g., "I thought a good paper could have evidence from secondary sources only, but now I think I need evidence from primary sources also"). Other times students realize the problem lies in products previously evaluated as adequate over the course of learning (e.g., "I thought I had a good plan, but I am not making progress on this assignment, so I need to rethink my plan"). Finally, there are times when students realize they need both to enact control for their current task and to make changes for future tasks (e.g., "Whenever I encounter difficulty, I tell myself I am stupid. That is not working for me, so I need to find a different way to handle challenging assignments").

The processes of SRL, monitoring and control, were derived from metacognition research; thus, the terminology most often used is *metacognitive* monitoring and control. However, students can monitor and control not just their cognition but all of the targets of SRL (i.e., cognition, metacognition, motivation, behavior, affect, and external factors), as well as learning products. Monitoring and control can be consciously invoked (e.g., "I'm going to self-test to see if I remember what I just read"), but this takes effort and time. As students acquire basic knowledge in a discipline, and as they become better at enacting SRL, they can automatize certain aspects of monitoring and control, such as judgments of understanding. This automation frees up working memory capacity and mental energy for engaging in the learning work. Nonetheless, monitoring still occurs, and students can become aware of a misfit between standards and products via metacognitive experiences. These metacognitive experiences are a primary driver of "bottom-up" aspects of SRL.[75]

Metacognitive Experiences

Over the course of completing academic tasks, students have metacognitive experiences, which are cues about learning.[70] Students can have a number of metacognitive experiences over the course of a learning task, and these experiences serve as moment-to-moment data about the task that can inform monitoring and control.[75] For example, students may experience a feeling of difficulty (i.e., confusion while reading) and then invoke conscious monitoring or control of their learning strategies. Sufficiently powerful or frequent feelings of difficulty can lead to adaptation of SRL targets, learning products, or previous products during SRL (e.g., plans). Likewise, feelings of fluency or understanding are metacognitive experiences that can serve as data to inform decisions to continue using automatic strategies and refrain from more extensive self-regulation.

One way researchers have studied metacognitive experiences, and their role in learning, is through the use of judgments of learning, where students are asked to estimate how well they would do on a test of the material they are learning. The degree to which students' estimations of their learning performance correlate with their actual test performance is called calibration. Recent research supports the existence of two separate but equally important calibration processes: knowing what one knows (i.e., sensitivity) and knowing what one does not know (i.e., specificity).[94] For example, poor performers, and people with low prior knowledge, often overestimate how well they will do on tests; in other words, they do not know what they do not know.[95,96] They also underestimate how much SRL they must enact to perform successfully.[97] This is particularly concerning because these metacognitive experiences are used to make decisions about continuing and changing learning; poor performers may have unwarranted confidence in their learning and decide to stop studying earlier than would be optimal, or they may continue with a maladaptive learning strategy. Research has shown that poorly calibrated students benefit from interventions teaching them to slow down their responses to metacognitive experiences. Calibration can be improved by taking time to think more deliberately about whether they understand and will be able to recall or use information.[98]

In addition, students, and people in general, often attend to the wrong cues when assessing learning. The ease with which people understand content is not a reliable predictor of whether they will be able to recall it at a later time. Likewise, people mistakenly believe that text that is made salient by the author, such as through bolding, italics, or bulleting, will be easier to remember than other kinds of text. Many people mistakenly think that studying once for a long period of time (i.e., massed learning) will result in better learning than studying more frequently for shorter periods of time (i.e., spaced learning).[5,99] Finally, these effects are prominent in both offline and online learning contexts; the ease and fluidity of online reading can often cause people to be overconfident in their ability to recall the material at a later time.[100] The solution to these common misperceptions and misconceptions about learning is to engage in desirable difficulties, such as by self-testing and spacing learning across multiple sessions. Calibration based upon spaced self-testing is far more reliable than when based upon metacognitive experiences such as ease of learning or saliency.[5,101]

Other metacognitive experiences include feelings of knowing, which are students' judgments of whether they know the answer when their initial attempt at recall fails.[70] Students are surprisingly good at these judgments; when they get the sense that they have learned something before, and will remember it on a later test, they usually do. The opposite is also true: students may know they have learned something before but think it unlikely they will remember it on a test, and they are often correct. Affective responses are another kind of metacognitive experience, and sometimes affect occurs before the realization of the cause of that affect (e.g., when frustration precedes a feeling of difficulty). All of these experiences are moment-to-moment events enabling bottom-up SRL. This bottom-up SRL during a task complements the top-down processing occurring during SRL, such as conscious efforts to self-regulate cognition, motivation, and other targets.

In sum, much of the process of SRL involves generating products and using metacognitive monitoring to compare those products to standards. Metacognitive control occurs when the fit is suboptimal and students decide to change some aspect of prior learning such as adapting targets of SRL, standards, or previous products of learning. These processes, when enacted consciously, can be quite effortful; therefore, there is value in automating them as much as possible. When automated, students rely on metacognitive experiences to trigger conscious monitoring and control, enabling decisions about when self-regulation should take place. There is relatively little known about how to train students to be more effective at automating metacognitive monitoring and control, interpreting their metacognitive experiences, or developing appropriate standards. Clearly, this is an area ripe for future research.

Summary of Models of SRL

What was presented here was an amalgamation of predominant models of SRL. Such a combination was possible because the models share substantial similarities, with many of their differences based in differing degrees of emphasis, as opposed to truly incompatible components. At their heart, models of SRL describe how students pursue desired academic goals by actively constructing, monitoring, and controlling the targets and products of SRL through a roughly ordered sequence of activities. It is tempting to argue that students should always enact SRL processes, for every learning task and context. However, students need to know not only how to enact effective SRL but also when and when not to deploy it. When students encounter an unfamiliar task, or experience unusual difficulty with an academic task they had previously mastered, they need the skill and will to inhibit their typical processing and invoke more effortful, but also more availing, SRL processes. On the other hand, reliance on automated learning processes, and the metacognitive experiences associated with learning, can be an effective and efficient strategy, particularly for students with high prior knowledge or experience with the learning task. It is unwise and impractical to enact effortful SRL for every academic task in formal and informal education, particularly given the energy it takes to self-regulate, and the many non-academic tasks also requiring students' self-regulation. These non-academic but nonetheless essential tasks in education have been studied in the literature on self-regulation.

SELF-REGULATION

Some goals are relatively easy to meet, and others are challenging. Some goals require a few moments of work, and others a lifetime. Some goals receive a tremendous amount of support from the outside world, and other goals are resisted by that world. Regardless of these differences, when people have to use conscious thought and effort to pursue a goal, such as when they encounter resistance or conflicts (e.g., obstacles and temptations), they are engaging in self-regulation.[14,33] Most researchers in cognitive, developmental, and social psychology define self-regulation as the active management of cognition, emotion, and behavior to achieve goals.[102] It is tempting to define successful self-regulation as the active pursuit of pro-social or academically normative goals, but to do so would be to limit the idea. People sometimes choose to pursue negative, harmful, or maladaptive goals, and doing so is an act of self-regulation. An underexplored aspect of self-regulation research involves understanding why some people choose to self-regulate toward maladaptive goals, and how to help them choose more beneficial ones.

Likewise, it is important to remember that people have and pursue many different kinds of goals, often simultaneously, including academic, social, interpersonal, financial, and personal goals. In some cases, students choose to engage in maladaptive academic behaviors not because they have a goal of failing in school but rather because they have decided that other goals, such as well-being goals,[36] are more important than academic ones and require self-regulation toward them despite the academic costs. These multiple goals, which are often salient and relevant in educational settings, are one important reason why a text on self-regulation in education such as this one cannot solely focus on SRL research. In education settings, students self-regulate based upon multiple goals, including academic and non-academic ones, with consequences for each.

Large amounts of research in cognitive, developmental, and social psychology, among other disciplines, have shown people's success at self-regulating predicts a wide variety of academic, health, and societal outcomes including measures of achievement such as grades and standardized test scores, health problems such as weight management and substance abuse, and issues of violence and financial success.[13,15,103] Different terms are more or less typical in the academic and non-academic literatures on these outcomes (e.g., willpower, self-control), but to a large extent they are all equivalent to, or include ideas encompassed by, the term "self-regulation."

Models of Self-Regulation

Most models of self-regulation can be grouped into two types. The first set of models describe how "lower-order" executive functions support and enable higher-order self-regulation.[13,47] The second set of models include self-regulation, or what some call self-control,[35] as a limited resource and illustrate how deploying self-regulation for one goal can have subsequent effects on future attempts at self-regulation. These models are not incompatible with each other, nor are they incompatible with models of SRL.

Models of Self-Regulation and Executive Functions

Self-regulation is often called a "higher-order" process, meaning that it is a complex mental process supported by numerous other more basic or "core" processes. Other examples of higher-order processes supported by these core processes include critical thinking, problem-solving, and reasoning.[87,88] The core processes are often called "executive functions." The executive functions literature is important to understand because individual differences in these core processes can influence the likelihood of people enacting higher-order processes such as self-regulation and the nature of that enactment.[13] For example, people who have atypically limited working memory capacity are more likely to struggle with higher-order processes like self-regulation, compared to their peers with more typical working memory capacity. However, it is important to remember that situations and contexts also affect the likelihood that a person enacts executive functions, as well as the nature of that enactment. The ability to control one's attention to stay on a diet is generally harder to enact successfully when surrounded by temptations, such as when working in a donut shop.[40]

There is particular importance to the term "executive" in executive functions. The "executive" term is typically used in developmental and cognitive psychology to indicate the function is intentional, conscious, and/or goal-directed. In the language of SRL, the term "executive" is akin to "top-down" regulation. Loud noises can cause people to automatically orient their attention and move toward the source of the noise, such as when an infant suddenly starts crying. This is not "executive" functioning. There is little that is intentional, conscious, or goal-directed in this functioning; people automatically respond in this way. In the language of SRL, automatic responses are one aspect of "bottom-up" regulation. On the other hand, caregivers who hear the noise but decide to let their child cry for a while, to determine whether the child could self-soothe back to sleep, are enacting "executive" functioning: they have to actively and effortfully inhibit the natural response to run to the child's aid, and instead they do something different in their pursuit of a desired goal, such as eventually getting a full night's sleep.

At this point in this text, it may feel redundant to state that there are debates in the academic literature regarding what executive functions are, which processes comprise executive functions, and which processes are subordinate or superordinate to other processes.[104] There is little need to delve into these debates here, but, when reading research on executive functions, it is important to be aware these differences exist. Such differences can influence how these processes are conceptualized, studied, and measured. The model of executive functions and self-regulation presented here is one of the more common and empirically supported ones.[13,47] In this model, there are three core executive functions mutually supporting each other, and in combination they support higher-order functions. These core executive functions are working memory, inhibition, and cognitive flexibility. Many researchers would include attention among these core executive functions,[105] but, in the model presented here, attention is the result of the three executive functions working in concert.

Working Memory

Working memory is akin to the conscious self; it is the part of memory involved in the conscious holding and manipulation of information. When people do complicated math problems in their head (e.g., $524 \times 22 = ?$), they are manipulating the information in their working memory. Working memory is different than sensory memory, which is a very brief memory store where most sensory perceptions (i.e., sights, sounds, tastes, smells, tactile feelings) are experienced, often not noticed, and then quickly forgotten. For example, students sitting in a classroom may be largely unaware of how their chair feels (e.g., comfortable, uncomfortable) unless something brings this feeling to their attention. Excessive pain can do this, such as in the case of a particularly poor chair, but most often students in classrooms have to direct their attention elsewhere, meaning the sensation of sitting in the chair enters and leaves their sensory memory without notice.

Attention enables perceptions to move from the sensory memory store to the short-term memory store. The short-term memory store is what people use when they wish to hold, but not manipulate, information. If students were told to pay attention to how their chair felt, and then asked to stand up so that they were no longer experiencing the sensation of the chair, they could still recall and report this sensation by rehearsing it in their sensory memory. Without continued concentration, though, this feeling would be forgotten, a process also known as "decaying." On the other hand, if the students were asked to compare how comfortable different chairs were, relative to each other, they would have to move the perception into their working memory. In their working memory, they can do more than just hold information; they can also manipulate it. Indeed, this manipulation is necessary for students to store the new information in their long-term memory. Manipulation can involve numerous processes such as organization and elaboration. During elaboration, people connect the new information they are learning to things in their long-term memory that they have learned previously. For example, students could compare how comfortable their current chair is compared to their favorite chair at home. Unlike long-term memory, which has no known limit to what it can hold, working memory is limited. Most people's working memory capacity falls within a relatively narrow band (e.g., seven plus or minus two pieces of information), and to date the majority of the empirical evidence indicates that people cannot increase their working memory capacity, despite the promises of various "cognitive training" businesses.[106]

There is a great deal more that can be said about working memory, including that it is actually comprised of two separate memory stores (i.e., verbal and nonverbal working memory), and there is much that can be said about how people can manipulate information in ways that allow for complex thinking and problem-solving. For the purposes of this text, beyond having a basic grasp of what it is and how it works, there are three important things to note about working memory. First, working memory is one of the three core executive functions. It is an "executive" function because, unlike sensory or long-term memory, it can be consciously controlled. People can choose to hold and manipulate information in their working memory, whereas they can only access what is experienced in their sensory memory, or what is stored in their long-term memory. Second, many researchers have argued that attention is really a product of working memory; in essence, when people pay attention to something, they are focusing their working memory on it. Third, individual differences in working memory capacity relate to the likelihood of enacting self-regulation, and the quality of that enactment. In general, those with greater working memory capacity are more likely to self-regulate, and more likely to do so effectively.

Inhibition

Whenever people replace an automatic response with something more thoughtful, they are enacting inhibition, also called executive control.[13] For example, many people's automatic, non-conscious response to being asked a question is to answer. If instead they choose to wait to see if someone else answers, perhaps because they think others in the room know more than they do about the question, they are enacting inhibition: they recognize and intentionally refrain from enacting their typical or automatic behavior, instead substituting something different that they think is more appropriate at the moment. People can inhibit many different kinds of natural responses, such as the instinct to eat a tempting dessert, the impulse to lash out at someone who wrongs them, or the inclination to believe whatever news is posted to their social media feed.

In early research on inhibition, the focus was on controlling behavior. Over the years, researchers have expanded the kinds of things that this executive function can inhibit and control, from behavior to cognition, attention, motivation, and emotions. It is important to note that the term "inhibition" really involves two processes: first stopping an automatic response and then starting a different one, even if that different one is something as simple as doing nothing. Sometimes people have to inhibit something they would typically do, such as reaching for a cookie after lunch, and sometimes they have to inhibit paying attention to some external stimulus or representation, such as trying to ignore a crying baby or loud talkers at a coffee shop. In each case, the inhibition involves not doing something more typical or automatic (e.g., reaching for a cookie, eavesdropping on loud talkers), and instead doing something requiring more effort (e.g., getting up from the table and ending lunch, focusing attention on something other than the loud talkers). People use inhibition both when they are trying to avoid responding a particular way (e.g., restraining the urge to call out answers in a classroom) as well as when they wish to maintain effortful activities (e.g., resisting the urge to check email when writing a paper for class).

Descriptions of inhibition often sound similar to descriptions of metacognitive monitoring and control, and indeed inhibition is a key core component of those higher-order processes. But inhibition involves only the recognition of the need for control (i.e., monitoring) and enactment of control; it does not include other aspects of metacognition such as planning or self-evaluation. Of course, individual differences in inhibition can affect whether, how well, and in what ways people enact self-regulation in education, and subsequent achievement.[15] These individual differences derive from biological factors (e.g., reactivity), learned factors (e.g., knowledge of effective delay of gratification strategies), and the effects of long-term exposure to environmental factors (e.g., growing up in an environment with numerous threats can make it more difficult to inhibit certain responses). The study of individual differences in how people react to stimuli—and engage self-regulation of affect, behavior, and attention—is called "temperament" research.[107] Some researchers have argued that people have a limited amount of energy for inhibition and that each act of inhibition depletes this store; when the store is empty, self-regulation is unlikely to occur (i.e., ego depletion models).[35,40] Such models will be discussed later in this chapter.

Cognitive Flexibility

The last core aspect of executive functioning is cognitive flexibility. Often called "shifting," "set shifting," "mental flexibility," or "task switching," cognitive flexibility includes not just switching between foci but also the ability to take other perspectives, both interpersonally and physically.[13] This executive function, which manifests in children's performance later than working memory or inhibitory control, plays a role in people's ability to think creatively, follow complex instructions requiring multiple steps, and apply previously learned strategies to novel problems.[103] Imagine parents taking their kids to a donut shop. When those parents refrain from ordering four donuts for themselves because they have set a weight-loss goal, that is inhibition. However, when they refrain from ordering those donuts but also think about how to talk to their kids about their decision, and how it relates to having a healthy body image, that is cognitive flexibility.

Summary of Models of Self-Regulation and Executive Functions

Despite some differences across models in terms of what the primary executive functions are (e.g., inclusion or exclusion of attention as a separate executive function), researchers concur executive functions form the core or foundation for higher-order processing, such as self-regulation. Some models include additional constructs beyond executive functions among the "core" or "foundational" aspects of cognition (e.g., temperament, personality),[14] and numerous models differ to some degree on whether self-regulation is a higher-order process, or whether various components of self-regulation (e.g., planning, self-monitoring) are the higher-order processes which in turn allow for self-regulation. Overall, however, executive functions research coalesces around a few key ideas including the importance of executive functions to higher-order processes such as self-regulation and problem-solving. In addition, executive functioning derives from both genetic and environmental factors, with the latter being the stronger influence. People's executive functioning ability can be influenced both by environmental factors as well as targeted intervention, both of which seem to be more influential in the early years of life. The majority of research has revealed few sex differences in executive functioning, with those studies finding differences revealing them to be small, and in favor of females.

Some researchers have made explicit connections between self-regulation and SRL models. For example, top-down regulatory processing is similar to the enactment of executive functions.[75] Likewise, people can be more or less likely to enact top-down executive functioning (e.g., inhibition) depending upon more automatic or "lower-level" aspects of executive functions, such as temperament or the degree to which someone has been achieving sufficient rest.[47] People's ability to enact executive functioning successfully can be improved through intervention and practice, similar to efforts to improve people's SRL ability. Nonetheless, more research is needed on the many likely ways executive functions relate to self-regulation and SRL.[103]

In sum, the broad outlines of self-regulation are clear: core executive functions must develop before higher-order self-regulation can occur, and differences in executive functioning can affect how people self-regulate toward multiple kinds of goals, including long-term and short-term goals, as well as academic and non-academic (e.g., well-being) goals.[15] The many goals students must manage in education (e.g., getting good grades, working amicably with teachers, making and maintaining friendships) can sometimes be overwhelming. In models of self-control, the second category of self-regulation models, people have limited resources for such management, which, when depleted, can affect the likelihood of successful self-regulation.

Models of Self-Control

Recall that there are many advantages to automated processing and action. Students who have automated successful strategies for familiar tasks can invoke them with far less effort and far less cost to their limited working memory. The need to actively self-regulate—whether it be learning, emotion, interpersonal relationships, or other activities—requires attention, energy, and time. Models of self-control focus on those costs and their consequences.[35] A prominent model of self-control focuses upon ego-depletion, or what some call resource-depletion. The idea in resource depletion is that each person has a certain amount of capacity for self-control, and, each time this capacity is tapped, some amount of that capacity is spent until a period of recuperation occurs. Research has shown that people who have to dip into their capacity for one task (e.g., resisting a piece of chocolate cake, inhibiting their use of an automatic learning strategy and enacting a new, unfamiliar one) subsequently have less capacity for future tasks of self-regulation. This implies that, when faced with multiple events requiring self-regulation, people's likelihood of successfully enacting self-regulation goes down with each event. People may vary in their capacity, as well as in how much a particular task of self-regulation costs them, but the basic mechanism is the same across individuals: self-control is a limited resource that decreases with each use, and it can be regained only after a period of rest uninterrupted by the need to self-regulate. This model provides a plausible explanation for why some students struggle to self-regulate in education: the more adversity a student faces, both inside and outside of the learning context, the less likely it is that successful self-regulation will occur. This model has considerable empirical evidence supporting it.[108]

Recently there have been suggestions that resource-depletion is not a fully accurate or replicable model of self-control.[109] One alternative, but similar, model of self-control is called the process model of self-control.[40] In this model, as in the resource-depletion model, each person has a finite capacity for self-control. However, this model differs in that it differentiates between the various ways people enact self-control, suggesting that some "cost" more than others. The model is easiest to describe using an example.

Imagine a student, Micah, whose automatic response when playing baseball at recess with a peer rival, Avery, is to angrily taunt him whenever they are involved in the same play (e.g., when Micah tags Avery out at second base). Suppose Micah had a goal of changing his behavior, and not taunting Avery any longer. When playing baseball with Avery, inhibiting the taunting response and replacing it with another, more adaptive response (e.g., instead of confronting Avery, Micah could simply tag him out and say nothing) would deplete some amount of Micah's resources for self-control. However, there are many other opportunities for Micah to act in ways that achieve the same goal prior to the moment of seeing Avery. These opportunities group into four broad categories that are roughly time-ordered. Early in the morning, Micah could anticipate whether Avery would be playing baseball that day, and, if it seemed likely, Micah could choose to do something else that would be unlikely to involve Avery, such as play basketball or talk with friends. This would achieve the same goal as inhibiting his anger toward Avery, but, according to the process model of self-control, choosing another situation costs less resources than having to actively inhibit a response once it has been cued.

On the other hand, it may be the case that the situation cannot be avoided; perhaps Micah has to play baseball with Avery because that is the only option available. He could choose to modify the situation by staying as far away from Avery as possible, such as by choosing to play outfield, where it is unlikely he would be close to Avery. This modification likely costs more resources than not playing baseball with Avery at all, but likely less than actively inhibiting the taunting response. Again, such a modification may not be possible due to the circumstances. In this case, the next best option, in terms of resource depletion, is for Micah to focus his attention elsewhere. He could tag Avery out and immediately throw the ball back the pitcher, focusing on getting ready for the next play. Finally, the last best option, compared to inhibiting the taunting response, would be to cognitively reframe the situation, such as by deciding that Avery is not worth the effort to taunt him. The key difference between the process model of self-control and other resource depletion models is that in the former there are hypothesized ways to achieve a goal with far less cost, whereas in the latter there is no differentiation between acts of self-control: they all cost the same.

Researchers continue to test and debate process models and other models of self-control, with Grit being a prominent example in both the academic and the layperson literatures.[110] Again, there are substantial overlaps between the various models of self-control, with some initial evidence that ideas such as Grit overlap substantially with more traditional concepts such as effort regulation.[111] Regardless, these models hold promise for understanding self-regulation in education, and they intuitively make some sense: the more often people have to self-regulate, and the more difficult that self-regulation is, the less likely it will be that they will have the energy to self-regulate in the future, barring a time of recuperation. Individual differences in executive functioning likely manifest in students' capacity and likelihood of enacting self-control.

Summary of Models of Self-Regulation

Readers interested in better understanding the relations among executive functions, self-regulation, and education will need to become familiar with these vast literatures in cognitive, developmental, and social psychology. Such literatures go by many names, including executive functions, self-regulation, temperament (i.e., broadly construed as manifest behaviors and typical dispositions resulting from complex interactions of biologically based reactivity with learned regulatory processing), and school readiness.[15] A historical review of these literatures reveals that their scope has broadened over time, from focusing on behavior and emotion as detrimental phenomena that must be controlled in the service of cognition (i.e., classic executive functions literature) to a view of behavior, cognition, motivation, and emotion as resources, with positive and negative aspects, that must be adaptively managed to optimize performance (i.e., more modern self-regulation literature).[15] As just one example, even seemingly positive emotions, such as excitement, likely relate to educational outcomes in an inverted U-shaped manner (i.e., Yerkes-Dodson curve), where too much or too little excitement is incapacitating, with moderate levels of excitement most likely to promote positive educational engagement and performance.

There is extensive research showing that young children differ in their readiness for the academic and social aspects of schooling. These differences predict both short-term and long-term outcomes in schools.[15] Such differences have been conceptualized in terms of core executive functions, which over time work together to form the foundation for higher-order processes such as self-regulation of cognition, emotion, and behavior. Some of the research on these higher-order processes has been done in educational contexts, but much of it has involved other personal, interpersonal, and societal goals. Self-control models have been created to explain why people can successfully self-regulate in certain circumstances but not others. Again, there is some resource depletion research involving educational contexts, but most of it has been done in other settings. Nonetheless, there are promising hypothetical connections between executive functioning and self-regulation, within and outside of educational settings. These connections include the idea that poor performance in terms of higher-order processing may be due, in part or in some circumstances, to developmental issues in terms of more core functions.

Clearly, the findings in the executive functions and self-regulation literatures have implications for how students develop SRL and their self-regulation in education overall.[47] There is a large number of instances when students must enact self-control in school, including when learning (e.g., focusing on an assignment rather than talking to a friend), socializing (e.g., managing friendships), and interacting with school systems (e.g., maintaining positive self-image during a disciplinary referral). Having models of how students do and do not successfully self-regulate in these instances allows educators, parents, and other adults in education the opportunity to assist students in what can be challenging acts of self-control, particularly for young children and adolescents who are still developing self-regulatory capacity and skills. Education researchers have posited how students develop SRL, and more work is needed to connect those models to developmental models of executive functions and self-regulation literatures. This is the subject of the next section.

DEVELOPMENT OF SELF-REGULATION IN EDUCATION

Despite qualifications regarding the need for more empirical, longitudinal research in self-regulation in education, current theory and empirical evidence suggest that many aspects of SRL—including defining tasks, planning, and self-reflection among other processes—depend upon adequate development of self-regulation more broadly, including lower-order or core processes such as executive functioning.[18,20] Executive functioning and self-regulation undergird SRL, whether it be the kinds of moment-to-moment metacognitive monitoring and control that leads to bottom-up regulation, or the more long-term self-regulation of learning and well-being goals enacted through top-down regulation, or the interpersonal aspects of SRL.[20,36,58] Likewise, the direction, intensity, and longevity of self-regulation in education depend upon people's facility at self-regulating their cognition, emotion, and behavior in reference to both academic and non-academic goals to maintain optimal performance.[18] Thankfully, there is strong congruence among developmental models of executive functioning, information processing, and the acquisition of SRL capacity.

Developmental Models of Executive Functioning

Developmental models of executive functioning, informed by empirical research with young children, show inhibition and working memory manifest in the first years of life and then increase in capacity across the preschool years and early childhood.[112,113] Kindergarten age serves as something of a pivot point, with increases in executive function capacity and performance allowing for the manifestation of higher-order processes such as the beginnings of cognitive flexibility and active self-regulation of cognition, emotion, and behavior. Around adolescence many students show a marked increase in cognitive flexibility, as well as improvements in planning, organizing, and strategic thinking skills. In general, self-regulatory capacity and ability increases a great deal from childhood through early adulthood.[102]

Given these findings, it may be tempting to assume typically developing students have sufficient ability to enact self-regulation in education successfully by middle school. However, neural structures critical to effective self-regulation continue to develop and mature through age 25.[103] Students develop the capability to engage in various aspects of self-regulation at various stages of life, but their likelihood of successfully enacting such self-regulation does not reach its highest level until well past traditional school age. Further, these developmental trends are just that, average trends, and individual development varies based upon not just biological variability but also the influence of caregiving and environment. In short, in the age-old debate of nature versus nurture as drivers of development, the answer is both, with a stronger role for the latter than the former.[102]

Dynamic systems theory paints a complex picture of self-regulatory development where individual differences (i.e., nature) can trigger environmental responses (i.e., nurture) such as parental or caregiver responses that further magnify the effect of those individual differences on functioning. For example, infants who are more sensitive to stimuli, or what is called "under-controlled" in the literature (i.e., less able to control their responses compared to their peers), may react in ways that lead caregivers to isolate them in an attempt to calm these children. Over time, this kind of environmental structuring can decrease the likelihood of these children getting opportunities to practice interacting with others, leading to shyness in childhood and a lack of practice in social behaviors and norms. The opposite can also be true, with infants who are less sensitive to stimuli (i.e., over-controlled) being given more opportunities to interact with the world, leading to gregariousness and well-honed interpersonal skills in childhood. As another example, children in resource-poor environments may take longer to develop typical levels of cognitive flexibility, due to a lack of stimuli demanding such executive functioning.[102]

Indeed, there is ample research that adults can positively influence development through the creation of warm and responsive environments with clear and consistent expectations. These environments encourage children's autonomy, which must be balanced by timely support when needed.

Research has shown that self-regulatory capacity benefits from parents and educators who are organized, clear regarding guidelines for behavior, and active in providing opportunities for students to practice executive functioning.[20] Considering the numerous ways individuals can differ in terms of their biology (e.g., differences in inhibition, working memory, reactivity) and the environments in which they develop (e.g., variations in kinds and number of caregivers, parenting style, availability of social and economic resources), educators should avoid assuming the average trends in development necessarily apply to individual students. Both students' current and previous environments can influence their likelihood of effectively self-regulating in a particular context. At the same time, it is likely unreasonable to expect students to display self-regulation in education performance that is well beyond what is typical of the average (e.g., asking kindergarteners to inhibit the use of games on a mobile device and instead focus on a learning application).

Information Processing Models of Development

Information processing theories of cognition and SRL, along with research into expertise development, illustrate how some students can indeed perform at levels well above what is typical for their peers.[24,114] So-called child prodigies often do have somewhat higher levels of innate ability than their peers (e.g., the 4-year-old violinist likely scores well on general assessments of dexterity and musicality), but the key distinguishers between competent and expert performance, at any age, are (a) the clarity of people's goals, (b) their motivation to improve, (c) whether they are able to receive feedback from coaches that balances manageable challenge with support, and (d) the amount of time they can spend practicing their craft. Experts' performance depends much more on the amount and quality of their deliberate practice than on their innate ability. Deliberate practice is differentiated from regular practice by the intense amount of concentration needed for the former, which even experts often describe as tiring and not very pleasurable. The mythical status of the commonly believed "born an expert" archetype (e.g., apocryphal stories of children who learned how to play an instrument with little to no training) is matched only by false belief in experts who do not continuously engage in hard work to improve their craft. Students who were born with atypically high levels of executive functioning, such as those students with more working memory capacity than is typical, may move from the novice levels of performance to competent ones more quickly than their peers, but research has shown the path from competent to expert performance depends much more upon the amount of deliberate practice a student enacts than individual differences in core executive functions.[115] Moving from novice to competent and eventual expert performance of self-regulation in education requires opportunities for deliberate practice of these skills.

Models of the Acquisition of Self-Regulation in Education

It is possible to integrate developmental and information processing theories of self-regulatory performance. In essence, individual differences can be bolstered, or ameliorated, through environmental influences, and one of those influences can be the degree to which a person can engage in deliberate practice. Deliberate practice is a mechanism for increasing performance and capacity for many necessary skills in education, and it likely paves the way for the acquisition of dependent higher-order processes. Human development puts some reasonable limits on the efficacy of deliberate practice:

asking most 5-year-olds to practice planning will likely lead to frustration on both the child and the teacher's part, but lower-order processes upon which planning depends (e.g., forethought, language) can be practiced and improved. In general, self-regulation in education requires students be able to use language, model the behaviors of others, and engage in forethought.[18] Language ability allows students to talk to others about the various aspects of SRL (e.g., What are good strategies for learning? What is an appropriate standard for this assignment? How did you do so well on that test?), but it also gives students a means of self-reflecting on their own cognition, metacognition, motivation, behavior, and affect. The ability to model others' behaviors allows students to learn from these people, and forethought enables the ability to predict what will happen as a result of SRL and adjust so that those outcomes are more likely to be positive rather than negative.

Zimmerman[17] has provided a model, based in social cognitive learning theory, of how skills are acquired and refined, with the end goal being a student's ability to enact SRL when enacting that skill. This model has been tested in terms of higher-order SRL processes, but further empirical work is needed to determine whether it also applies to more fundamental processes. Learning to write an argumentative paper is a good example of this model. Novices to argumentative writing are unlikely to have the knowledge or automated strategies to self-regulate their learning when enacting such a skill. Asking students to monitor and control their argumentative writing is challenging when they have not acquired or automated the skill. Zimmerman's model demonstrates how students acquire both the skill, in this case argumentative writing, and the capacity for actively self-regulating their learning when enacting this skill.

At the first level, observation, students must be exposed to models of varying quality, with the goal of identifying the qualitative differences in their performance. In the case of writing argumentative papers, students could be exposed to good and poor argumentative papers, with the goal of learning how to discriminate between strong and weak arguments. Ideally this discrimination will involve multiple standards, including not just those related to the final product (e.g., a strong counterargument is presented and effectively rebutted) but also those related to the process of writing the paper (e.g., self-regulating motivation to begin the task, proper planning). Often at this level the student's motivation must be externally regulated, thus illustrating the importance of having teachers or coaches. Deliberate practice research aligns with the features of this level, particularly the finding that early phases of performance acquisition require targeted feedback and encouragement. Students at this level can become frustrated when they increase their effort but see little difference in performance. It can be helpful to have a teacher or coach to assure the student that the hard work will pay off in the future.

Students achieve the next level of acquisition, emulation, when they are able to mirror the general form of the models presented. In the case of the argumentative writing example, students have reached the emulation level when they can produce a strong argument with assistance, requiring feedback to achieve the desired level of quality. At this level, students are unlikely to transfer the skill to other domains or contexts. They adhere closely to the model's performance, and they still need the model to complete the task. Nonetheless, this represents real progress in skill acquisition: the student can generate a product, which can serve as a feedback tool and a target for motivational reinforcement (i.e., "You did it! Now let's figure out how to do it better, on your own").

Movement into the third level of Zimmerman's model, self-control, requires the student to be able to perform the skill outside of the presence of the model. Such a performance requires automation of the skill, so that working memory capacity is available for transferring the skill to a new topic, domain, or context. Deliberate practice continues to play a key role in movement through and beyond this level, but now students have internalized representations of model performance and can self-evaluate the degree to which they have met these standards. At this level, students can write argumentative papers, but they must continue to refine and improve the process of doing so. Critically, at this point most students can self-motivate, which is important because the focus of the deliberate practice must move from evaluations of the product to evaluations of the process as well. A focus on process and the desire to continue improving that process require the ability to motivate oneself and enact volition strategies. Indeed, many students end their deliberate practice at this level, particularly if they expect to enact the skill in only a limited range of contexts, which they have already mastered.

The final level of the development of skills, called self-regulation, is typified by the full automation of the skill and the ability to adapt the skill to changing personal and contextual factors. Automation is essential at this level because the focus is on using the skill to achieve desired goals rather than simply improving skill performance. Motivation to continue deliberate practice at this level usually involves assessments of the students' self-efficacy for self-regulating the use of the skill. It is at this level that the student has moved fully beyond dependence upon models or coaches. However, this is also the point when students can move on to higher-order skills requiring the skill they just learned to self-regulate. So, in the writing example, students may use their ability to write an argumentative paper to begin acquiring the skill of writing a research proposal. Again, students begin this process at the observation level, relying on the automation of argumentative writing to free working memory capacity, and motivational and volitional resources, for the purpose of acquiring research proposal skills.

As with most models of change over time, Zimmerman's levels should be seen as depictions of typical development, but not an invariant, mandated process. Some students move quickly through a level; others can stall for quite some time. Students who reach the self-regulation level for a particular skill may not always enact it as such, depending upon individual and contextual factors such as motivation or time pressures. Finally, the deliberate practice literature indicates that expert performance requires continued effortful reflection, practice, and effort. In some sense, if people are not working to improve upon their expertise, they are beginning down the path of losing it.[115]

SUMMARY OF MODELS OF SELF-REGULATION IN EDUCATION

The purpose of this chapter was to outline a synthetic perspective on self-regulation in education, which spans literature and research on SRL and self-regulation. The various SRL models were combined by highlighting the targets (i.e., cognition, metacognitive knowledge, motivation, behavior, affect, external environments), the phases (i.e., before, during, and after learning), and the processes of SRL (i.e., monitoring, control, and metacognitive experiences). The implicit assumptions of these models were made explicit, such as the recognition that oftentimes SRL is not needed, particularly when an effective and efficient plan for completing an academic task has been automatized. When students lack such a plan, they should thoughtfully enact both top-down and bottom-up regulation, using the former to best prepare themselves before learning and the latter to adjust to the specific demands of the academic task as their work unfolds. Of course, students must engage in both academic and non-academic tasks in formal and informal education, and models of self-regulation provide a broader perspective on how students can set productive goals and maintain optimal levels of energy both inside and outside of the classroom. It is important for educators, parents, and other adults in education to remember that self-regulation in education requires adaptive goals, strategies, and support for both academic and non-academic tasks. The development of the capacity and ability to engage in self-regulation in education develops over time, through a complex interaction of natural and environmental factors, hopefully regulated in positive ways by students and adults alike. The vast majority of students have sufficient innate ability to successfully self-regulate in education, but they often need support as they learn to do so. The next chapter includes reviews of how self-regulation in education relates to a number of academic and non-academic outcomes in schooling, which provides support for the importance of developing effective interventions to help students better self-regulate in education, which is the focus of Chapter 4.

Three

How Does Self-Regulation in Education Relate to Learning and Achievement?

Research has shown school readiness and success depend upon students' ability to self-regulate in education.[7,8,15,31,116] Students' self-regulation in education has both direct effects upon achievement (e.g., students who can regulate their volition are more likely to persist when studying) as well as indirect effects (e.g., students who can regulate their emotions are more likely to have positive relations with peers and teachers). General trends in the empirical literature (e.g., self-regulation plays an important role in academic achievement, above and beyond the effect of IQ) are similar in both the SRL and the self-regulation literatures, but there is much more to learn about self-regulation in education, in terms of both theory and practice.

Another area of scholarship that is proving ripe with new ideas and research directions involves studying the disciplinary-specific aspects of self-regulation in education.[31,49,50,117] Researchers in this area have focused primarily on differences in how frequently students enact self-regulation in education (e.g., planning, monitoring) across disciplines, and less upon whether those processes differ in their (a) likelihood of being enacted, (b) relevance, or (c) nature across disciplines. Nonetheless, there is growing interest in how people engage in SRL differently across disciplines such as mathematics, reading, writing, science, and history.

The last context worth exploring in contemporary research involves the ways in which SRL is enacted and supported within technology-based learning environments.[118] The growing prominence of technology in modern life has paralleled the increased interest in understanding how people self-regulate within these contexts. Likewise, the unique affordances and challenges of technology-based learning environments have led to a dramatic increase in research on how to teach, support, and measure SRL within such contexts.[119] By the end of this chapter, the "problem space" of self-regulation in contexts will be well-defined, with numerous directions for future research identified.

RELATIONS BETWEEN SRL AND ACHIEVEMENT

The empirical literature on relations between SRL and achievement falls into two large groups. Researchers continue to explore how learning strategy use and instruction affect academic achievement outcomes. Indeed, strategies are the tools for learning, yet there is growing evidence that people's intuitions about which tools are most effective are often incorrect.[5] The second group of empirical studies includes an extremely large body of research involving investigations of how the targets and processes of SRL relate to academic achievement. Some of these studies focus on a few of these targets or processes, and some focus on many. Some of these studies involve determining whether the use of particular SRL strategies or skills predicts learning, whereas others involve experimental investigations of various means of instructing SRL and subsequent effects on academic achievement. This second group of studies is vast, which makes synthesizing its results both challenging and potentially rewarding. Meta-analyses have been conducted to do this challenging work and have revealed several strong, empirically supported claims about what aspects of SRL relate to academic achievement and how they can be fostered.

Learning Strategies

There is a great deal of overlap between research on SRL and research on learning strategies, particularly given that SRL developed from the combination of learning strategies, metacognition, motivation, and social cognition research. Readers interested in more depth regarding learning strategies research should consult *Strategic Processing in Education* (Dinsmore, in prep/this series). In short, research into cognition and achievement has revealed that people learn more effectively when they engage deeply with content, connecting that content to their prior knowledge.[67] For example, simply reading and rereading a text does not promote retention and performance nearly as well as reading and then self-testing (i.e., when people ask themselves questions about the material). Further, such self-testing is more efficient when people force themselves to recall information (e.g., using flash cards) versus simply recognizing information (e.g., answering multiple choice questions where the correct answer needs only to be recognized among other incorrect options). Also, self-testing seems to be more effective after a short delay, such as when people read material, take a ten-minute break, and then return to self-test. Finally, conducting all learning and self-testing in one or a few study sessions right before an exam (i.e., cramming) is less effective for long-term retention and performance than spacing out learning and studying material over a longer period of time, with greater frequency. Spacing learning and studying can actually be more time-efficient than cramming, as more-frequent but shorter study periods can produce better performance than less-frequent, longer study periods. Additional details on the efficacy and efficiency of specific learning strategies are beyond the scope of this text, but suffice it to say that much of the conventional wisdom on how to learn is incorrect, suggesting the need for rigorous, systematic, empirically informed instruction on learning strategies.[5] These findings on domain-general learning strategies will be supplemented later in this chapter with findings regarding domain-specific strategies in mathematics, reading, writing, science, and history.

Meta-analyses of SRL

The empirical literature on SRL is, frankly, enormous. Trying to read it all, and then synthesize it, is a herculean task. Thankfully, scholars have conducted meta-analyses of the literature that do this work. In short, a meta-analysis is a statistical combination and summary of all of the empirical literature on a relationship of interest, such as "what is the correlation between frequency of SRL behaviors and academic achievement?" or "what is the overall effect of SRL interventions, compared to control conditions, on academic achievement?" These meta-analyses involve finding every relevant and methodologically sound study and then combining their findings to estimate an overall average effect (e.g., SRL interventions produce medium-to-large effects on learning performance, compared to control conditions),[8] giving a better answer to the question than any one study could do alone.

Of course, the accuracy of a meta-analysis depends upon the quality of the studies included; the "garbage in, garbage out" rule applies. However, meta-analyses allow for several ways of investigating whether the studies differ in quality, whether the pool of studies suffers from some kind of systematic bias (e.g., overestimation of relationships because studies showing no relationship are less likely to be published), and whether there are important qualifiers of the relationships found in the literature. This last point is particularly important: meta-analyses can reveal whether the relationship of interest varies based upon a number of theoretical, practical, or methodological factors. Using an example from outside of the self-regulation research, a meta-analysis revealed small-group classroom discourse improves student comprehension, compared to control conditions (e.g., whole-class discussion).[120] However, this overall effect was qualified by the type of small-group discussion model and the student population.

In short, small-group discourse interventions focused on both understanding the text and student connections to that text (e.g., affective responses) outperformed those focusing on just understanding the text. Further, the effects of these small-group discourse interventions seemed to be stronger for students with lower ability compared to those with average or high ability. Therefore, the type of small-group discourse intervention and the students receiving it both "qualified"—or, in the parlance of meta-analysis, "moderated"—the overall average effect found when combining all the relevant studies in the literature (for more information, see *Classroom Discourse in Education*).[121] Thus, meta-analyses provide not just a statistical summary of the empirical literature on a question of interest; they also provide information on how that summary varies across numerous qualifiers, which can inform how interventions are designed and targeted to particular populations and contexts.

To date, there have been four major meta-analyses of the SRL literature.[7,8,43,122] Each was conducted somewhat differently, but their results largely support one another. Training students on SRL leads to moderate to large gains on academic performance, compared to control group students who do not receive SRL training. Further, direct instruction of cognitive and metacognitive strategies, when bolstered with frequent opportunities for students to practice and receive feedback on those strategies, leads to greater achievement gains than more implicit methods of teaching SRL, such as modeling cognitive or metacognitive strategy use without direct explanation or instruction.[123] These findings align with other research into teacher-student scaffolding interactions, where it has been found that effective scaffolding must include diagnosis of the student's current level of functioning followed by the provision of new knowledge and skills that push the student without overwhelming them.

Support during students' practice of this new knowledge and the new skills must gradually be faded over time transferring more and more responsibility for implementation to the student.[124] These general findings on scaffolding align well with models of the development of SRL.[17]

Not surprisingly, longer interventions lead to greater gains in academic performance than shorter ones. Likewise, feedback appears to be a key aspect of successful SRL interventions. SRL processes often take a great deal of time to internalize and automate; therefore, educators should be prepared to engage in ongoing training with numerous opportunities for students to get feedback regarding their progress, including explicit feedback on what and how they can improve. Further, these meta-analyses indicated a need for extensive training and support for teachers tasked with implementing SRL interventions. The efficacy of these interventions requires they be implemented with sufficient fidelity (i.e., adherence to the design of the intervention) and dosage (i.e., frequency of training). Such findings align with research showing the limits of short "train the teacher" programs with no ongoing coaching or support.[125,126]

There were numerous important qualifiers of these effects. Use of metacognitive processes was a stronger predictor of achievement than use of cognitive processes, across primary and secondary students. This makes some sense, because after accounting for other factors such as knowledge of strategies, which increases over K–12 schooling, students' knowledge of and ability to engage in metacognitive processing likely differentiates more- and less-successful students.[7] Nonetheless, knowledge and use of cognitive strategies was a significant predictor of achievement; it was simply a less powerful predictor than metacognitive strategy knowledge and use. Further, the type of cognitive strategy matters as well. Higher-order cognitive strategies—such as identifying main ideas, making inferences about the content, and elaborating upon what was being learned—had stronger correlations with performance than lower-order cognitive strategies such as rereading or memorization. Taken together, the meta-analyses showed empirical support for many of the conceptual claims in SRL models: the use of high-quality cognitive strategies involving elaboration and other ways of connecting new content to prior knowledge, when combined with metacognitive processing involving planning, monitoring, and evaluation, are most likely to lead to high achievement. Learners must know not only what strategies they should use but also when and how to use them.

Despite the overall effectiveness of SRL training interventions across K–12 education, there is some evidence that the focus of those interventions should differ between primary and secondary school settings. Primary school students seemed to benefit more from interventions designed from either a social cognitive or a motivational perspective, whereas secondary students benefitted from interventions based in metacognitive models of SRL. This suggests SRL interventions with younger students should focus on bolstering self-efficacy and motivation through direct instruction of efficient and effective cognitive strategies, such as constructive note-taking and self-testing. On the other hand, older students, who already have knowledge of such strategies, seem to benefit from direct instruction in metacognitive strategies such as monitoring progress toward goals and calibration, as well as training on how to use metacognitive reflection to learn when such strategies are best used. Interventions involving cooperative or collaborative learning, as opposed to individuals learning on their own, have produced mixed results, with some meta-analyses finding these types of interventions more powerful, and others finding them less powerful. Numerous researchers have speculated that the quality of the collaboration fostered is the key differentiator. Cooperative or collaborative learning is not necessarily natural for students, nor is it necessarily easy to teach without training.[127] It seems likely that SRL interventions involving collaboration would benefit from the incorporation of research into how to effectively teach and foster small-group collaboration.[45,128]

Finally, for adults, self-efficacy and the quality of the goals people set seem to be strong predictors of performance. Adults who think they can be successful at a task are indeed more likely to be successful, which is not a surprising outcome. Likewise, when adults set challenging goals, they achieve more than adults who set easier goals.[43] Such goals may enhance people's ability to self-regulate their motivation and volition, which have been shown to be strong predictors of academic achievement in college.[129]

Summary

Meta-analyses have supported the models of SRL that have arisen from early research on learning strategies, metacognition, motivation, and social cognition. Such models suggest the importance of direct instruction of high-quality learning strategies, followed by opportunities to practice and reflect upon those strategies' use so that metacognitive knowledge can be developed. These models are necessarily broad and general, however, and there is still much to learn about how SRL is enacted in educational contexts and how to teach students to do so more effectively. In particular, much more research is needed into how SRL depends upon, and interacts with, students' self-regulatory ability. SRL and self-regulation pull from the same mental resources, and challenges in one aspect of self-regulation in education can leave little capacity left for enacting other aspects.

RELATIONS BETWEEN SELF-REGULATION, SCHOOL READINESS, AND ACHIEVEMENT

General self-regulatory ability—including the ability to set goals, monitor, and control cognition, behavior, and emotion—predicts both short-term and long-term achievement in school (i.e., through Grade 6), even after controlling for IQ and demographics.[102,130] Current models of school readiness suggest an interactive relationship, where initial self-regulatory ability and academic performance upon entrance to educational environments interact with factors in those environments (e.g., teachers, peers) to create either virtuous or vicious cycles, which in turn predict later engagement in learning and academic performance. When students are able to regulate their goal striving, behavior, and emotion, this often leads to more positive interactions with teachers and peers, which in turn promotes more academic engagement and better academic performance. Likewise, low levels of self-regulatory capacity or skills can lead to difficult or even infrequent interactions with peers and teachers, with subsequent negative effects on engagement and performance.

Recent research has revealed the toxic influence of childhood stress upon initial self-regulatory performance, illustrating how students who experience extreme difficulties at home (e.g., poverty, abuse) are often less likely to successfully self-regulate at school, which in turn increases the likelihood of a vicious cycle of poor social interactions, lack of engagement, and poor academic performance.[131] Importantly, these cycles are descriptions of what happens on average, and they should not be understood as definitive or mandated for any individual student. Some students show remarkable resilience to factors that, in general, predict poor self-regulatory performance. Nonetheless, education systems should proactively create environments that help students self-regulate, rather than counting on such resilience. Thankfully, self-regulation is a malleable skill, amenable to classroom and school-wide interventions. Educators and other adults in schools can take actions to foster effective self-regulation.[130]

Executive Functions, Self-Regulation, and Education

The executive functions of working memory, inhibition, and cognitive flexibility all support higher-order functions, including self-regulation as well as other processes that are the subject of other books in this series (e.g., strategic processing). Theoretical relations between core executive functions and school readiness have been born out in the literature, showing that these core executive functions are more predictive of school readiness than general intelligence.[15,132] Indeed, in the past, school readiness was defined as literacy and basic mathematical skills, but a strong argument can be made that executive functioning and self-regulation are key aspects of school readiness.[15] Further, people's facility in enacting core executive functions is related to numerous educational outcomes, including academic achievement in reading and math, as well as overall grade point average.[76] Such findings have held for Caucasian, Hispanic, and African American samples. There is also growing evidence that executive functioning predicts reading and mathematics performance not just in the early years of schooling but throughout K–12 education.[132]

In terms of the acquisition of higher-order processes, the literature has also shown that executive functions are particularly important when initially learning a higher-order skill (e.g., reasoning), but as those skills are mastered individual differences in executive functioning become less influential.[13] In essence, this literature suggests one goal of education should be to help learners sufficiently master skills to the point where day-to-day changes in environmental stressors have less of an effect upon performance, due to automation and subsequent less dependence upon executive functioning. In addition, there is a clear need for longitudinal research on how early interventions for executive functioning affect self-regulation and, subsequently, educational performance and outcomes.

On the other hand, there is evidence of important nuances to the established relations between executive functioning and achievement. For example, kindergartners' ability to enact executive control positively predicts performance, as would be expected, but this skill is particularly important when children feel low, not high, levels of anger. In these instances, children with strong executive control skills can regulate their anger and focus on achievement. Children with poor executive control skills can have difficulty regulating, and subsequently have fewer resources available for achievement, resulting in a greater likelihood of maladaptive relations with peers and teachers. Interestingly, the utility of executive control ability decreases when children experience high levels of anger; at these levels, few students are able to effectively regulate their emotions.[107] Such findings illustrate the complex nature of real-world self-regulation: even the most adept self-regulators can struggle when pressures are high, such as when experiencing high levels of anger. It may be that teachers view it as normal when students with high levels of anger require support self-regulating but that they look negatively upon students who fail to successfully self-regulate when experiencing low levels of anger.

The quality of support students receive, and perceive, affects their likelihood of successful self-regulation, both in the moment and in the future. Much of the self-regulation literature is focused on young children; therefore, parents, caregivers, teachers, and other adults are the most often referenced support givers. However, peers can also provide support, or undermine it. Developmentally, there is a greater need for support from others in the early stages of life, with this need decreasing slowly over time as an individual's capacity for self-regulation increases. Increased capacity for self-regulation is partly developmental but also strongly influenced by the kinds of support the individual experiences over the lifetime. In general, warm, responsive relationships involving appropriate amounts of support and challenge tend to foster increased self-regulatory capacity.[102] Again, the quality of experienced support, or lack thereof, is not the sole determiner of an individual's likelihood of successfully self-regulating, but there is no doubt it is a powerful factor.[15]

Another nuance in the relations between executive functioning and academic achievement concerns the home environment. Recent research has shown chaotic households, defined as those households with high levels of disorganization, do not directly affect the development of executive functioning or self-regulation performance in kindergarten. Instead, they seem to affect parents' ability to be responsive to children, and scaffold their children's developing executive functioning and self-regulatory abilities.[130] Parents in disorganized households are less likely to have time or resources to help students develop effective self-regulatory skills, which in turn makes these children less likely to be ready for school. These findings further illuminate the critical role parents play in self-regulatory development and make a strong case for initiatives that help parents create environments where they have the resources to provide guidance and support for the development of key school readiness skills such as self-regulation.[131]

Classroom and school-wide environments can be shaped to increase the likelihood of successful student self-regulation. In general, research indicates that environments that are organized, safe, and supportive increase the likelihood of children enacting successful self-regulation while engaging in novel or challenging work.[20,130] Given that young children's working memory is not yet at its maximum, it is particularly important to automate as much as possible in early grades so that students can focus their limited resources on learning and self-regulation. This suggests the benefits of clear, familiar, and well-structured routines for commonplace classroom activities (e.g., explicit student-friendly procedures for engaging in solo and group work).

At the same time, students' feelings of legitimate autonomy are important predictors of effective self-regulation as well.[133] The keys to legitimate feelings of autonomy are not simply opportunities for choice but rather opportunities for meaningful choices. Incidental choices, such as allowing students the choice of what color pen to use for a writing assignment, do not foster feelings of autonomy. At the other end of the spectrum, extreme amounts of autonomy (i.e., pure discovery learning)[134] do not provide sufficient support for students to engage in challenging work. Instead, opportunities for meaningful choices should come within larger structures of support, such as when students can choose the topic of an argumentative essay, or when they can collaborate with their teacher to co-construct classroom policies at the beginning of an academic year. The research suggests that autonomy, and subsequent self-regulation, flourishes within an environment with a balance of challenge and support, with the recognition that such balance will change over time as students increase their capacity for performance.

Finally, despite being less studied than classroom interventions for self-regulation, the literature suggests the importance of extrapolating the characteristics of self-regulation-supporting classroom environments to the entire school. Incongruity between the goals, supports, and opportunities in the classroom and the larger school context decrease the likely efficacy of the former and diminish the possibilities of the latter. Ideally, self-regulatory support and instruction should be consistent and encouraged throughout the educational environment, so students receive a consistent, reinforcing message.[131]

There is great potential for the application of research in self-regulation within schools. For example, a recent meta-analysis showed interventions designed to foster people's ability to monitor their progress toward goals led to greater likelihood of goal attainment, because such interventions increased the frequency of monitoring by a large amount.[135] Unfortunately, the authors could not find studies in education settings where both goal attainment and frequency of monitoring progress toward goals were measured. Therefore, the established relations in this meta-analysis have not been examined in terms of educational goals. Nonetheless, these findings suggest that one exciting direction for future research involves translating these interventions for monitoring progress toward goals to educational settings, where non-experimental research has found such behaviors related to achievement outcomes.[136]

Summary

The empirical literature on self-regulation reveals it to be an important predictor of school readiness and academic success, whose effect upon performance throughout schooling is subject to dynamic interactions between personal, environmental, and contextual factors. In particular, how teachers and other adults in education respond to students' ability to self-regulate their cognition, emotions, and behavior can have a dramatic effect on academic performance over time. That said, students do not experience schooling in an omnibus, generalized way. Instead, students interact with different teachers, peers, and academic subjects over the course of a school day. These students' likelihood of successfully enacting self-regulation in education, and how they do so, can vary dramatically across academic disciplines and contexts.

RESEARCH ON DISCIPLINARY DIFFERENCES IN SELF-REGULATION IN EDUCATION

Despite early calls for more discipline-specific investigations of SRL,[137] only recently have researchers begun investigating which aspects of SRL might vary by academic subject (e.g., mathematics, science, history).[50,138] Such work shares similarities with investigations of context in self-regulation research[105] and the situated learning movement[48] in that it calls into question the degree to which SRL functioning can be attributed to individuals, as opposed to the dynamic interaction of people and environments. In the SRL literature, empirical research varies from investigations of whether SRL differs in degree across domains (e.g., a person is more likely to self-regulate in one discipline, less in another), as well as in type (e.g., self-regulation in science involves fundamentally different strategies than self-regulation in writing).

Mathematics

Meta-analyses of relations between various aspects of SRL (i.e., metacognitive strategies, motivation, etc.) and mathematics academic achievement have revealed substantial correlations, within both primary and secondary school samples, although effect sizes were larger for primary students.[7,8,122] Interventions designed to foster SRL in the mathematics vary, but there is evidence that explicit instruction of SRL processes (e.g., teaching students what metacognitive strategies are, when to use them) leads to measurable effects, whereas implicit instruction (e.g., teachers modeling SRL processes, but not explaining what they are or how to do them) leads to much smaller effects.[123] Such findings have persisted even when researchers take into account general measures of IQ.[139] Interestingly, one study showed that metacognitive monitoring and control do not predict mathematics performance among second graders, once differences in executive functioning are taken into account.[140] It may be the case that, among younger students, the core executive functions play a larger role in performance, with higher-order metacognition knowledge and skills playing a larger role among older students, and in courses with more advanced mathematical concepts.

The literature on SRL in mathematics, overall, has provided evidence of substantial relations between SRL and performance, but there is a need for more interventions specifically geared toward teaching mathematical reasoning strategies, in addition to general metacognitive and SRL skills (e.g., planning, monitoring, self-questioning).[141] Likewise, there is initial evidence that teachers' explicit modeling and scaffolding of SRL and math-specific strategies can bolster mathematics performance and attitudes.[142] However, more research is needed regarding whether there are mathematics-specific SRL strategies and, if so, whether they contribute to mathematics understanding and performance beyond more general SRL strategies.

Reading

Meta-analyses have shown that current SRL interventions in reading produce stronger effects in secondary students, compared to primary students. This does not mean that SRL interventions related to reading should only be conducted with secondary students. Rather, it may be that SRL interventions on reading must differ in focus, and it seems likely that there is more to be learned about what primary students need in terms of SRL interventions for reading performance. On the other hand, reading has long been a focus of metacognition research.

There is a great deal of research into how students monitor their comprehension while reading. The research began in the 1960s and formed the foundation of what has become work on metacognitive experiences.[143] Early research utilized relatively simple texts (e.g., lists of word pairs to be memorized), but more recently researchers have studied students' comprehension of larger text passages, with this area of scholarship being called metacomprehension research. The distinctive elements of research on reading and SRL, as opposed to SRL in other disciplines, are the foci on calibration, the broad array of metacognitive experiences identified when students calibrate, and how students use those metacognitive experiences to monitor their learning. These metacognitive experiences include feelings of knowing (e.g., "I see the next section of the text is on Abraham Lincoln. I bet I would do well on a test of Abraham Lincoln"), judgments of learning (e.g., "I think I would get 80 percent on a test of what I just read"), and ease of processing judgments (e.g., "This is pretty easy for me to read"). Such metacognitive experiences have varying degrees of utility as cues for whether material should be reread or studied again before a test, with delayed judgments of learning the best indicators.[101] The delay is important; immediate judgments of learning after learning are more likely to be inaccurate, with the theory being that the read text is still activated in working memory and therefore biasing estimates toward overconfidence. There has been a great deal of research on other cues students use to predict test performance with many shown to be unreliable,[5] and there is evidence even preschoolers can accurately calibrate their learning with their metacognitive experiences, provided they are asked to delay, and given appropriately worded prompts.[101]

There is far less research on how students enact metacognitive control after a metacognitive experience indicates likely poor performance on a test. Initial research suggests students do a better job of enacting appropriate control after metacognitive monitoring (e.g., selecting parts of texts they are not yet able to recall or understand) when they are asked to engage in elaboration strategies while reading.[144] Likewise, there is evidence that students who do enact a change in strategies after realizing they did not understand what they read outperform those who keep enacting the same strategy.[145] Further, explicit instruction on reading comprehension strategies (i.e., activating prior knowledge when reading the title and headings of a text, self-questioning during reading, organizing ideas from the text graphically) has shown to lead to better reading comprehension than implicit or no instruction.[146]

Finally, there is evidence that giving students a test and immediately providing them with feedback and results helps students choose which sections of text to restudy more effectively than having them engage in certain forms of self-monitoring, such as asking them to generate relevant keywords after reading.[147] Such findings do not mean that self-monitoring is a poor choice of strategy, but rather they mean that such monitoring may be more effective when using the results of self-testing rather than feelings of difficulty or other cues on their own.[148] Overall, interventions designed to teach students metacognitive strategies have shown slightly higher than average effects for English and Language Arts performance outcomes, compared to other subjects. The goal of future intervention research continues to be student automation of metacognitive monitoring and control, using appropriate cues, so that students make good decisions about what to study. In addition, there is a need for more research into how students calibrate their learning with other kinds of text, such as graphical and online representations.

Writing

Often, educators and researchers group reading and writing together, but in fact there are different models of mental processing, and different empirical literatures, for these two higher-order skills. The majority of reading research has been conducted within a metacognition framework, whereas writing has been informed by SRL and self-regulation literatures.[149,150] Models of writing mirror the phases of SRL, focusing on how students should (1) plan what they want to say and how to produce it, (2) spend time writing the text, and then (3) engage in revision to hone their message. Further, modern models of writing include explicit connections between higher-order cognitive writing processes and executive functioning, including attention, working memory, and inhibitory control.[151]

Many SRL in writing interventions have produced large average effect sizes, with a recent meta-analysis showing strong effects for interventions involving goal setting, self-evaluative standards, mental imagery to promote creativity, and planning and revision, as well as combinations of all of these processes.[152] One example of an effective writing intervention that has evolved over time due to rigorous long-running research is the self-regulated strategy development writing model and intervention.[151] This intervention has produced large effect sizes across over 100 empirical studies, and this intervention has led to effects upon not only writing quality but also knowledge of writing and self-efficacy. Further, researchers have shown this intervention promotes generalization of gains in writing performance across contexts.

The specifics of this intervention will be reviewed in Chapter 4, as an example of an effective SRL intervention. Here, the key point is strong effects were found when ideas from SRL and self-regulation literature were specifically adapted and refined over time based upon empirical research, for the writing context.

Science

Many empirical SRL studies have involved students engaging in science-learning tasks.[153] There is evidence that SRL plays an important role in science learning, particularly in terms of motivation to engage in science and the persistence needed to acquire scientific understanding.[154] The relatively recent shift in emphasis in science education, from learning scientific facts to acquiring scientific inquiry and argumentation skills, has led to a greater need for students to be able to self-regulate their learning.[11,155] This shift in the goals of science education has been mirrored by a shift in research on SRL and metacognition in science away from domain-general knowledge and skills to discipline-specific SRL in biology, chemistry, and physics, among other sciences.[156]

Yet, only a portion of the research on SRL in science has involved examining what distinguishes SRL in science from SRL in other domains. There have been arguments that scientific reasoning and understanding includes a number of science-specific strategies including ways of engaging in analogical, deductive, inductive, and abductive reasoning. Further, science involves a number of complex ideas that are often contrary to popular understanding (e.g., the cause of the seasons is not due to the Earth getting closer to the sun, as is commonly believed), with some of these ideas directly contradicting deeply held beliefs (e.g., evolution versus creationism). Researchers have argued that these scientific ideas contradicting intuitive or conventional wisdom make substantial demands on students, which can subsequently lead to cognitive dissonance and negative emotions requiring self-regulation.[158,159] There is some evidence that positive emotions strengthen the positive relation between SRL and science outcomes, whereas negative emotions can greatly weaken or even overwhelm this relation.

Whether the roles of cognitive dissonance and emotion, as moderators of the relationship between SRL and performance, are unique to science or not remains unclear. Nonetheless, the research evidence suggests that these self-regulatory targets, as well as the domain-specific strategies necessary for conducting science, play a particularly important role in science.[50] Unsurprisingly, intervention work has also shown greater benefits for instructing both science-specific strategies and SRL together, rather than either one separately.[160,161] Students learning science content online or with technology seem to benefit from metacognitive prompts cuing them to plan, monitor, or evaluate their learning, as well as more general cues to connect what they are reading to prior knowledge.[156,157] Unfortunately, much of the research on science and SRL has been conducted with older students, and less is known about how elementary school students enact SRL to learn science.[161] Likewise, much of the intervention work in science has involved a focus on skill building rather than instruction in metacognitive knowledge about tasks or strategies, or how to interpret metacognitive experiences in science.[156]

History

There has been relatively little research into how self-regulation might occur differently in history contexts as opposed to other academic subjects.[162,163] Historical reasoning and inquiry include a number of seemingly history-specific strategies and skills including how to gather evidence and sources, evaluating the credibility of those sources, and corroborating information across these sources. Likewise, historical understanding requires establishing the chronology of sources and events, taking the perspective of individuals at that time in history to understand their actions (i.e., historical perspective taking), and then making inferences based upon the evidence to establish explanations and causal structures for both individual events as well as larger trends and themes in human history.[62,63] There is some evidence for planning as an important process for learning in history, which is unfortunate given that often students do not engage in much planning.[162] Successful students have been found to be more likely to monitor their use of strategies and self-question, compared to their less-successful peers.[50] Research into how to scaffold students to enact SRL in history is in its early stages.[164]

Summary of Disciplinary Differences

Despite being a relatively new area of scholarship, there is growing evidence showing both common features and distinct differences in SRL across disciplines.[49] The phases of learning, and the metacognitive processing occurring in those phases, appear to be similar across disciplines. Students who are new to a discipline or task should define tasks, set goals, make plans, and regulate their motivation before learning. Likewise, during learning, monitoring and controlling understanding and progress seem to be important processes. Adaptive attributions for performance and regulation of emotion are also seemingly common beneficial endeavors after learning.[68] What is less clear is whether the roles of executive functioning and self-regulation vary across academic disciplines; this is an area in need of research.

Nonetheless, the actual strategies students should enact during learning do seem to vary by discipline and task. The literature on disciplinary differences in self-regulation in education points to some commonalities, in that there seems to be both domain-general and domain-specific learning strategies, both of which predict performance. Whether it be historical reasoning, scientific experimentation, self-questioning in reading, or working backward and forward in mathematics, these domain-specific learning strategies seem to be important predictors of success and should be taught alongside more domain-general self-regulatory processes such as monitoring understanding and responding to metacognitive experiences. The roles of planning and self-reflection appear to be underresearched both within and across academic domains. What does seem most common across work in the disciplines is that students benefit from direct instruction in both domain-specific and domain-general learning and SRL strategies. Such strategies are becoming more and more important as students gain increasing access to an enormous variety of non-curated sources via the Internet. Any discussion of self-regulation, in general, would be incomplete without a focus on how educational computing is changing the nature of self-regulation in education, and its importance.

SELF-REGULATION IN EDUCATIONAL COMPUTING CONTEXTS

It may seem odd to devote an entire section of this book to self-regulation with computers, but there is growing evidence that for all of the amazing advances they have brought about, computers are not a panacea; they can be both a powerful affordance and a serious detriment to students and their learning.[165] Computers have enabled educators to provide students with a number of differing representations of complex phenomena and opportunities to interact with those representations in a myriad of ways, which research shows fosters understanding.[166] For example, educators have developed hypermedia learning environments to illustrate connections between concepts and provide support for understanding by allowing students to explore ideas and terms with which they are unfamiliar. Simulations have allowed students to dissect animals and learn anatomy in ways that were cost-prohibitive or morally untenable in the past. Digital games can be used to teach students concepts in a familiar and incentivized format, such as by using game features like "leveling up" to encourage students to explore ideas in deeper way.[167] Advances in computerized tutoring have enabled educators to provide large numbers of students with individualized instruction and feedback, tailored to their prior knowledge and skills, with the ability to fade support over time as the student shows increased performance.[168] The extreme malleability and cost efficiency of computers have opened doors for educators and students to a degree unheard of since the invention of the printing press.

At the same time, these same computers have brought with them new challenges. For example, many computer-based learning environments, such as the Internet, are not formally reviewed or curated, requiring students to determine which links are relevant and worth exploring, versus which are tangential, irrelevant but interesting, or even dangerous.[136] The provision of multiple representations requires that students be able to integrate those representations into a coherent understanding, a challenging task for students, particularly those with little prior knowledge of the topic.[169] Digital educational games have potential, but many students have reported that there is a substantial difference between a game that teaches versus an instructional lesson with game-like features (i.e., "gamification"), with the former often far more engaging than the latter. Computerized tutoring has been shown to lead to cognitive benefits,[170] but the effects upon student motivation and interest remain unclear.[171,172]

One key to students' successful leverage of the affordances of computers, and avoidance of their challenges, is the degree to which students can effectively self-regulate how they learn with them.[118,119,173] The literature on self-regulation in educational computing contexts forms two groups: one concerning the self-regulatory challenges of having access to computers while learning, and the other regarding how students can be best positioned to take advantage of all that computers can do. The latter group includes both how students can be empowered to use computers effectively and how computers can model and foster effective use.[174]

Self-Regulation and Computers

Pursuing academic goals with computers, such as research for a paper or using a simulation, can be difficult given the many temptations of computer games and the Internet. Indeed, much has been written about the distractions of social media and the digital world, and about their effects upon learning.[175] Increased access and accessibility bring with them the need to self-regulate so that desired goals, particularly academic ones, can be met. This is true even for "digital natives"—i.e., the students who were born recently enough to have never lived without computers and modern technology.[176] Despite proclamations and speculations in the popular press, today's students are not fundamentally different than students of the past.[177] They may be more facile with web browsers, social media, or mobile apps than their parents, but research has shown that these knowledge and skills do not mean that these students are naturally effective at learning with computers.

Perhaps proliferated by today's media, many students feel they can multitask, which is the process of switching frequently back and forth among multiple activities requiring their conscious attention. Multitasking behaviors are so commonplace that many students believe they can do it with little to no cost to their learning. Some adults, including parents, argue that today's students "need" to multitask to learn.[176] Nonetheless, the research evidence on multitasking is clear: multitasking leads to decreases in learning performance and increases in the time necessary to complete tasks, and this holds for younger and older students, as well as those who multitask frequently versus those who do so less frequently. The human brain is a serial processor: it can focus its attention, its conscious thought, on just one thing at a time. Switching conscious attention from one task to another, rapidly, leads to decreased performance in each because the mind must take some time to recall what was being done on that task and what needs to happen next.[178,179]

Setting up systems and safeguards to decrease the likelihood of being distracted or tempted when using computers is necessary given self-regulation resource depletion models.[35,40] There are studies showing that students who experience something that depletes their ego, including playing videos games, are more likely to seek out things and behaviors they find pleasurable.[180,181] This may be adaptive for students who find their learning task pleasurable, but many tasks are not as much fun as watching TV or browsing the Internet; therefore, it is important that people reserve as much of their mental resources as possible, so it can be spent on self-regulating learning, particularly with computers.[182] Indeed, in one study, observations of college students in a large lecture classroom revealed that up to two-thirds of laptop use was off-task, such as browsing the Internet or shopping, suggesting widespread failure to self-regulate effectively.[183]

Research has shown that tablet apps with simple interfaces could be successfully used by students regardless of their executive functioning skill, but apps with complex interfaces posed serious challenges to students with lower levels of executive functioning, who struggled to find and attend to important information.[184] E-textbooks allow students to carry around a library of books in their pocket and annotate them in helpful ways. At the same time, there is research showing that it takes students longer to read e-textbooks compared to physical textbooks, perhaps due to technology distractions.[185]

Even laptop use in the classroom brings with it advantages and challenges. Research has shown that students can capture much more of what they see and hear during a lecture using a laptop compared to a pen and pencil, but the difference in the volume of notes does not translate into better learning. Rather, in one study, students who took notes using a pen and paper outperformed laptop note-takers, regardless of whether they were tested immediately after taking notes or after some time to study.[66] The researchers found that laptop users were more likely to take verbatim notes, whereas pen and paper users had to summarize and synthesize what they saw and heard. The finding that the process of summarizing and synthesizing leads to better retention than verbatim note-taking aligns with information-processing theories of cognition. Connecting new information to prior knowledge, through summarizing, synthesizing, and elaboration, is a more powerful strategy than simply transcribing that information.[67]

Finally, the potentially negative effects of laptops in the classroom extend beyond the individual user. Researchers have found that when an individual student uses a laptop for off-task behavior during a class (e.g., shopping online), not only does that student's learning suffer, but so does the learning of those peers who can see the laptop screen. Dubbed the "second-hand smoke effect," this finding, while in need of replication, does suggest that computers can distract more than just the students who use them. Whether laptops and other mobile devices should be banned from classrooms is a hotly debated topic (e.g., some students need to use a laptop due to disabilities, so banning them means "outing" those students in ways they may not wish), but, regardless, the self-regulatory challenges are clear. Self-regulatory skill and will, including delay of gratification and inhibition, are needed to avoid these challenges and capitalize upon the huge potential of technology for learning.

Self-Regulated Learning with Computers

The literature on the role of SRL in computer use is growing at a tremendous rate. There is ample evidence that SRL knowledge and skills mediate the relationship between computer use and learning.[17] In other words, students who have effective SRL knowledge and skills can take advantage of the affordances of computers to increase their learning beyond what they could do without computers, whereas students who lack SRL knowledge and skills often struggle to use computers to learn. Students with higher amounts of prior knowledge or self-efficacy are more likely to enact SRL while learning with computers, with the frequency and quality of that use predicting learning outcomes.[186,187]

Research has shown that students who enact effective cognitive and metacognitive strategies, as well as those with adaptive motivation and help-seeking tendencies, are more likely to learn with computers, whether they involve hypermedia, simulations, or games.[118,119,187,188] Determining which strategies are effective with computers depends to some degree upon the content being learned (e.g., history strategies differ from science strategies, as discussed elsewhere in this chapter) and the prior knowledge of the student. Students with less prior knowledge tend to use basic knowledge acquisition strategies (e.g., taking notes, rereading) so that they can become familiar with the nomenclature and fundamentals of the content. Students with more prior knowledge tend to use more effective, and specific, organization and elaboration strategies to connect what they are learning to their prior knowledge, make inferences about what they are reading, and ask questions about the content. In both cases, students' motivation to engage with the content, and their ability to manage their volition, matter. Knowledge of effective strategies (i.e., skill) is not enough; students must also have the motivation (i.e., will) to enact those strategies and persist through difficulties.[169,189,190]

Computer-based learning environments can also be structured in ways that increase the likelihood that students enact SRL. For example, one of the advantages of simulations is that they allow users a high degree of control. This control can be quite useful for students who have the skill and will to enact SRL, but this control can be equally challenging for students who lack SRL skills and will.[187] Therefore, simulations, and other computer-based learning environments, should be designed in ways that take into account student characteristics. At minimum, such environments should indicate to educators their target audience (e.g., novices in an area, more-experienced students, etc.). An even more powerful way to address differences in student users' characteristics is to design computers to be adaptive.[153]

There has been a great deal of recent work on creating computer-based learning environments that can diagnose students' understanding and adapt the content accordingly. For example, early versions of Microsoft's Encarta program were basically a hyperlink version of an encyclopedia. It presented the same content, in the same representations, to all students. Research showed that students' prior knowledge and SRL knowledge and skill predicted whether they would learn from this computer-based learning environment.[118] In addition, there was evidence that, compared to unassisted learning conditions, adaptive human scaffolding (i.e., effective diagnosis of the students' understanding, followed by direct instruction of key ideas or next steps, followed by fading of support as students showed they understood) led to learning gains for students who lacked prior knowledge or SRL skills.[162] Such studies paved the way for the creation of computer-based tutors who could mimic human scaffolding.

Current work on computer-based tutors goes by many names including adaptive learning technologies[174] and intelligent tutoring systems.[170] These systems, which are often limited to a relatively small corpus of content compared to static environments such as Encarta, vary in terms of whether they can support students' content understanding, SRL, or both. Nonetheless, progress is being made in automating the kinds of support that a human tutor might provide. For example, students' path through the hyperlinks in the environment can reveal whether they are focusing on key ideas or getting confused, lost, or unmotivated. Likewise, students' use of tools, such as highlighting or note-pad features, can be used to determine whether students are effectively self-regulating their learning.[99] Some environments even periodically prompt student users with questions using their answers to determine which content to show the students next. Research into types of prompts has revealed that mixed prompts for both cognitive and metacognitive strategy use, rather than prompts for only one or the other type, have the strongest effect upon learning and performance.[100,191,192]

Finally, the vast wealth of data collected by computer-based learning environments (e.g., hyperlinks clicked, notes

made, answers to prompted questions) can be used to identify aspects of SRL to model and scaffold for students.[99,193,194]
There is interesting work being done with animated pedagogical agents, which are computerized helpers who pop up
on screen to suggest or teach students various ideas or skills,
when the system determines it necessary.[195] Such agents can
provide anything from a quick suggestion (e.g., "You may
want to reread the section on quadratics given that you got
that question wrong") to more extensive modeling and scaffolding (e.g., "I think it would really help you if you started
using the note-pad feature. Let me show you how it works
and why it can be helpful . . ."). Some agents can even diagnose students' emotions during learning and prompt in ways
that help, or hinder, self-regulation of those emotions.[196]
At the moment, adaptive computer-based learning environments are a relatively new area of research, so their scope
is often limited to a few concepts or academic disciplines.
Nonetheless, they hold great potential for producing at scale
what many educators do now in a one-on-one manner: teach
students how to effectively self-regulate their learning with
computers.

SUMMARY OF EMPIRICAL LITERATURE ON
SELF-REGULATION IN EDUCATION

The prominence of self-regulation in education research, and
its growing influence upon educational standards, illustrates
its importance to education.[12] Students' readiness for school,
their interactions with others, and their academic performance
are all directly and indirectly affected by their facility with
self-regulation and SRL. The great promise of self-regulation
in education research is that by studying how it relates to
success in school, researchers and educators will be able to
craft interventions and environments capable of teaching and

supporting positive self-regulation. Such research must go beyond domain-general investigations, however, and begin to identify the ways in which self-regulation in education varies by context, including disciplinary (i.e., history, science, mathematics), classroom (i.e., presence or absence of computers), and social (i.e., various types of collaborative groups) contexts. Truly powerful and scalable interventions will require understanding what should and should not be taught to students about self-regulation in education and to what degree, if at all, educators should expect that instruction to generalize across contexts.

Four

How Can Educators Help Students Become Better Self-Regulators in Education?

After adopting the view of self-regulation in education as a multidimensional topic spanning the informed and intentional pursuit of relevant academic and well-being goals, and reviewing research showing how self-regulation in education predicts a number of positive academic outcomes, the next logical step involves investigating how to help students more effectively enact self-regulation in education and achieve their associated academic and social goals. To some degree, students learn how to self-regulate in education by observing others. However, developmental models of self-regulation have stressed two key ways teachers, caregivers, and other adults can facilitate the acquisition of self-regulatory capacity: direct instruction of knowledge and skills, and scaffolding approaches to support the internalization and mastery of these knowledge and skills.[131] Likewise, in his internalization model of SRL, Zimmerman[17] described a similar process of how specific knowledge and skills are observed and integrated into an individual's repertoire of behavior, moving from highly externally or co-regulated to self-regulated enactment.

In this chapter, rather than recapitulating how students typically develop self-regulation in education knowledge, skills, and dispositions, the focus will be upon targeted interventions shown to have a differential effect upon the acquisition and use of effective self-regulation in education and for learning. There is more research on self-regulation interventions for younger students than there is SRL research; therefore, it makes sense to begin the chapter with the former. Likewise, there is more research on SRL interventions with older students than there is on self-regulation interventions with those students. However, students are not the only people in formal and informal education environments who can benefit from self-regulation in education. Indeed, there is a growing literature on how educators themselves can train their peers to implement self-regulation in education interventions and how teachers have dual roles as self-regulated learners themselves as well as teachers of SRL.

INTERVENTIONS TARGETING SELF-REGULATION

Self-regulation is a higher-order process that is built upon core executive functioning. The latter supports the former; therefore, interventions targeting one often either directly or indirectly target the other. Nonetheless, there are some differences in these intervention literatures, primarily in terms of the kinds of claims that are made and their efficacy. Likewise, interventions that foster more effective performance in one aspect of self-regulation may free up resources to spend on other aspects, leading to changes in self-regulation beyond the focus of the intervention. Finally, one specific kind of self-regulation intervention, mental contrasting and implementation intentions interventions, will be reviewed as an exemplar of this area of research.

Executive Functioning

Despite evidence that executive functions are strong predictors of school readiness and performance, providing evidence of causal relationships, and then affecting those relationships through interventions, has proven far more challenging.[197] Interventions designed to improve executive functioning have a mixed history of performance, likely due to the wide variation in their implementation and the kinds of outcomes measured. In short, despite their appeal, short, compartmentalized interventions (e.g., brain games) designed to enhance particular components of executive functioning (e.g., working memory capacity, inhibition) have not led to practically significant changes in executive functioning beyond those functions targeted and have not led to measureable gains in academic performance.[198]

The findings for longer-term, more comprehensive, curriculum-based executive functioning interventions are more encouraging.[199] Efficacious interventions share several key characteristics. First, they are not isolated tasks or games that come and go over short periods of time; instead they are infused throughout the curriculum and school day. For example, both formal learning and recreational time can be structured to involve role-playing, which taps executive functions such as cognitive flexibility and inhibition of a student's normal response through the enactment of a different one. As another example, providing students with language and behaviors they can use when upset (e.g., pause, reflect, use your words), and structuring numerous opportunities for practicing these words and behaviors, can help them learn to manage emotions.

Second, successful comprehensive, curriculum-based executive functioning interventions are designed such that as children develop competence in executive functioning for particular tasks or scenarios, the challenge is gradually increased, so students internalize and build on what they have learned. Educators and adults should be frequently and informally assessing students' executive functioning and then providing scaffolded support that fades over time as students show increased capacity for successfully enacting new skills. When those skills become automated, the challenge, as well as the support, should be increased so that the scaffolding and fading cycle can begin again. Third, effective interventions require extensive educator training and support. Relatively short-term professional development, done outside of the education context, is unlikely to sufficiently prepare or support educators for effective implementation.[126] Fourth, interventions should not target particular aspects of self-regulatory performance while also challenging other aspects, such as when interventions on how to delay gratification also require young students to sit still for long periods of time listening to lectures on delay strategies.

Another effective class of executive functioning intervention involves training educators and adults to create supportive educational environments.[200] Such environments can be shaped to foster better executive functioning and increase the likelihood students enact it when needed. For example, educators can normalize executive functions, such as inhibition and cognitive flexibility, as important parts of classroom education. Talking openly and explicitly about the challenges and benefits of executive functioning gives students their own language for reflection upon these skills, and it makes it less likely that students experience shame or frustration when they are unsuccessful at enacting them. Classrooms that reduce the likelihood of negative affect (e.g., stress, frustration) and increase the likelihood of positive affect (e.g., pride, joy) also increase the likelihood that students will have the resources necessary for effortful enactment of executive functions. This includes acknowledgment and acceptance of what happens not only in the classroom but beyond it as well. Educators who display authentic care for students, and their life situations, are more likely to encourage students' feelings of belongingness and autonomy, which make effective executive functioning more likely.[133]

In sum, short interventions for building executive functioning (e.g., computerized brain games) seem to have little effect, but they may be effective as one component of a broader intervention strategy for addressing executive functioning challenges. Such a broader strategy requires long-term training and support of educators who implement executive functioning instruction, support, and fading throughout the curriculum. These implementations must be targeted with the appropriate amount of challenge and support so that students are learning, practicing, and automating knowledge and skill within their zone of proximal development. Likewise, the classroom environment should be one in which executive functioning is an explicit, tangible outcome so that students feel appropriate amounts of pride and accomplishment as they improve, and are less likely to experience feelings of shame when challenges overwhelm their current capacity. Such environments can ameliorate some of the disadvantages at-risk children experience before they arrive in formal schooling, and build a foundation for more complex self-regulatory functioning.[130]

Self-Regulation

Self-regulation interventions, focused on higher-order processing than executive functions training, are often called socio-emotional curricula or interventions and involve direct instruction of strategies for planning, monitoring, and controlling cognition, emotion, or behavior. Most self-regulation interventions also involve trained educators who act as effective co-regulators of such regulation. There is a large body of research evidence on such interventions, with the majority focused on direct skills instruction with pre-school and elementary school populations. Less is known about how to foster and support effective self-regulation in middle school and high school, which is unfortunate given the evidence that physiological and social changes during these years exert a great deal of stress upon students' academic and social well-being.[131]

Nonetheless, effective self-regulation interventions share many common characteristics. These interventions help students learn effective strategies for motivation, volition, and emotion management (e.g., self-rewarding, future goal orientations, positive causal attributions, growth mindsets). Also, these interventions help students identify their strengths and weaknesses and then choose effective strategies for managing them. Students who struggle with overreactivity can be taught to recognize when their emotions arise and how to channel them effectively. In essence, these interventions help students develop knowledge of themselves, regulation strategies, and the conditions under which they should use various strategies. This kind of self-reflection and understanding may be easier for older students to do on their own, but even younger students can be taught to better understand how they react in various situations and what they can do to better enact monitoring and control.

Self-regulation interventions are prolonged and integrated into the school curriculum, are implemented by teachers with significant training and support, and occur within educational environments with warm, responsive adults who communicate clear and consistent expectations.[20] These adults provide appropriate levels of challenge and support, fading such support as students show increased capacity. The structure of classrooms can be a support when it is organized, warm, and focused on respecting all learners.[201] As students display automaticity with self-regulatory skills (e.g., successfully collaborating with friends on an academic task), educators can increase the challenge and support so that students can build upon their knowledge and skills (e.g., asking students to collaborate on academic tasks with peers they do not know as well). Making social and emotional learning an explicit desired outcome of education helps students to both focus their energy on this work and experience less negative affect when they do not successfully self-regulate their interactions with others.[202] Students at-risk for self-regulatory difficulties seem to benefit most from such classrooms, although all students thrive in positive, non-threatening learning environments.[200,203]

Mental Contrasting and Implementation Intentions

Direct instruction of self-regulatory strategies is an effective component of most interventions; therefore, it is helpful to review one such strategy intervention in detail. One of the most empirically supported general strategies for self-regulation, regardless of context, combines two separate strategies into a single process: mental contrasting and implementation intentions.[33] Mental contrasting involves asking students to picture their future goal (e.g., making friends in a new school) and then identify any anticipated barriers or difficulties they may encounter while pursuing that goal (e.g., struggling to start conversations, being rejected). This mental contrasting helps students identify potential barriers, and it has had led to improved help-seeking, goal-pursuit, and academic performance. In essence, mental contrasting is a structured and informative way of comparing present and desired future states, and it is more effective than simply thinking about what it would be like to achieve a desired goal. However, self-efficacy can moderate the effect of mental contrasting. When people have high self-efficacy for their future goal, mental contrasting leads to more goal-setting, planning, and persistence. However, people with low self-efficacy often switch to other goals as a result of mental contrasting; therefore, students' self-efficacy should be assessed and bolstered, if necessary, before mental contrasting.

The effects of mental contrasting, and their persistence, can be amplified by adding implementation intentions to the intervention. Implementation intentions are "if . . . then" statements about how to overcome obstacles, such as those identified during mental contrasting, and have been shown to have a substantial effect upon performance in many aspects of life, including learning.[204] An example of implementation intention, based upon the previous mental contrasting example about making friends, would be: "If I feel shy when trying to speak to someone new, I will take a deep breath and then introduce myself." Conceptualizing implementation intentions before beginning the task makes students more likely to self-regulate effectively when confronted with obstacles. In essence, they automate certain aspects of control, thus making that control less costly to enact. Research has shown that the combination of mental contrasting and implementation intentions (e.g., "I want to make new friends, so if I feel shy when trying to speak to someone, I will take a deep breath and then ask them how they are doing") is more efficacious in terms of goal persistence and achievement than either one on its own. This general self-regulation strategy has proven effective in terms of academic achievement as well as other aspects of life-functioning such as health and pro-social goals. More research is needed regarding the relative contributions to the learning of mental contrasting and implementation intentions versus other aspects of SRL (e.g., calibration, discipline-specific strategies). However, it certainly seems plausible that these self-regulatory strategies could be combined with, or tailored to, self-regulating learning.[205]

INTERVENTIONS TARGETING SELF-REGULATED LEARNING

Many of the same principles for effective interventions in self-regulation apply for intervening upon students' SRL as well. Indeed, students can exert more effort on self-regulating their learning when they are in an environment where they feel supported in terms of their socio-emotional interactions, and vice versa. There are numerous SRL interventions documented in the literature, but most share some common characteristics.

General Findings regarding SRL Interventions

There is growing empirical evidence that students as young as kindergarteners can be taught to self-regulate their learning and that making such knowledge and skills explicit goals of education leads to tangible benefits.[20] Unfortunately, there is also compelling evidence that educators rarely make SRL knowledge, skills, and dispositions an explicit aspect of their instruction, instead relying on modeling without explanation, or not addressing them at all.[123] This inattention to SRL as a relevant, important educational outcome increases over the course of schooling, meaning that students who fail to receive such instruction and support early in their formal academic career are unlikely to receive it in sufficient amounts to "catch up" in their later years. This scenario leads to persistent educational inequalities where students who, for whatever reasons, were fortunate enough to acquire SRL knowledge, skills, and dispositions early in their educational career have a persistent and significant advantage over those students who, again for whatever reasons, did not receive such instruction. Such trends make SRL interventions an important tool in any educator's toolbox.

Most successful SRL interventions follow a common pattern of fading support as students display increased facility with the content.[38] Direct, explicit instruction of SRL processes is required. Such instruction should acknowledge that effective SRL involves processing before, during, and after learning. Many students do not think of the before-and-after aspects of learning; therefore, educators should directly instruct processes for each phase and all targets of SRL. Strategy instruction research has revealed the importance of teaching not just what to do to effectively self-regulate (i.e., declarative and procedural knowledge) but also when and why to do it (i.e., conditional knowledge). Recent research has suggested that metacognitive strategies (e.g., delayed judgments of learning) should be taught abstractly first but then contextualized and frequently practiced within a discipline (e.g., science).[206] Explicit and direct instruction in SRL should not occur separately from instruction in content; rather, it is most effective when taught in the context of students' instruction in subjects such as reading, mathematics, or history.[207] The tangible benefits of SRL, particularly in recognition of the significant costs, must be emphasized. Finally, students benefit from practicing what they have learned with tasks that require SRL, such as ones requiring critical thinking, argumentation, or deep conceptual understanding. It is difficult to practice SRL with simplistic tasks or with tasks where the majority of students have already automated effective and efficient plans and strategies. Likewise, when appropriate, the assessments associated with challenging tasks should provide feedback not only on task performance but also on SRL performance, and how both can be improved.

Educators should not depend upon direct instruction alone. Such instruction should be followed quickly by modeling the technique and then providing opportunities for students to practice with their peers. During practice, feedback is essential, from both educators and peers. The important role of feedback highlights the need for educators to create environments where such feedback is welcome, and leads to positive rather than negative affect. Such environments are characterized by several factors. First, social interaction among students for the purposes of cooperative learning should be a fundamental aspect of the learning environment rather than an unusual activity reserved solely for practicing and receiving feedback on SRL. Likewise, educators who focus on the constructed nature of knowledge, rather than portraying knowledge as solely a received good, are more likely to create environments where SRL is seen as valuable because students understand that they have to exert effort to create their own meaning of the material. SRL is learned and more likely to be transferred when it is taught in the context of relevant disciplinary knowledge, adjusted to students' current prior knowledge, and practiced with the explicit goal of automating its execution.

Finally, self-appraisal and reflection are important SRL skills that should be taught and explicitly endorsed.[38] SRL is effortful, and, after learning, students' remaining resources for continued effortful practice may be low. Nonetheless, after the completion of a learning task, educators should find ways to support students' reflection about themselves, their learning, and the outcomes they achieved. Rubrics are one tool to help students reflect on their task definition; comparing the rubric to the students' task definition can reveal what differences exist, which is the first step toward improving students' ability to match their task definitions to their teachers' intentions. Such insights, and practice achieving them, are necessary for students to accurately and effectively target long-term refinement of their SRL. Such long-term refinement can include setting attainable yet challenging goals, focusing on mastery of desired knowledge rather than comparisons of performance with others, managing time to allow for the pursuit of both academic and well-being goals, and monitoring and controlling progress toward these goals.[38,208]

Self-Regulated Strategy Development

The self-regulated strategy development (SRSD) program is one of the most effective and most thoroughly investigated interventions in education.[209,210] Designed to foster effective writing among both typically performing and special needs student populations, it produces very large effects across a wide variety of writing outcomes (e.g., quantity, quality, and self-efficacy of writing), also showing evidence that it can be implemented with fidelity by trained teachers who can serve both as the people directly providing the intervention and as the coaches for their peers who are learning to implement it. Thus, the SRSD is a useful example of an SRL intervention because it has strong effects and it is something that practitioners can implement and share with a reasonable amount of training.

SRSD instruction aligns with the overall literature on effective instruction of SRL. For example, writing knowledge and strategies are directly instructed, with trained educators targeting the instruction to students' needs and capacities. Students learn not only the declarative and procedural knowledge necessary to enact the strategies but also the conditional knowledge needed to know when and why to implement strategies; such instruction increases the likelihood of application and transfer. Instruction progresses as students display internalization of the strategies, with different rates of progress accommodated through a combination of group and one-on-one instruction, practice, and feedback.

There are six stages to SRSD instruction of a strategy, and within each stage students learn, use, evaluate, and refine the strategy. The first stage involves activating and learning relevant background knowledge about writing and self-regulation, such as analyzing model texts and reflecting upon how self-talk can either impede or facilitate writing performance. In the second stage, students and teachers discuss the characteristics of effective writing processes, including both general and genre-specific elements. Strategy instruction, spanning declarative, procedural, and conditional knowledge, is explicit and is coupled with motivational support and a focus on setting challenging but reachable goals for the acquisition and continued use of strategies. In the next stage, the teachers model the strategy, as well as how to plan, monitor, and evaluate its efficacy. Teachers also model how to self-regulate their attention, emotion, and motivation through reflection and self-talk. Over the course of the next two stages, students acquire and automate the strategy through a process of scaffolding that provides high levels of support initially, which then fades over time as students show increased facility with the strategy. The last stage of strategy instruction is characterized by students' ability to implement the strategy independently, at which time teachers push students to apply the strategy in novel contexts to promote generalization. Finally, despite the emphasis on ordered stages, SRSD instruction explicitly allows for students to skip or repeat stages as needed. The SRSD model clearly follows instructional practices shown to lead to effective acquisition and use of learning strategies and SRL processing in general.[123]

Practice-Based Professional Development

Recently, the creators of the SRSD intervention have studied how teachers could implement SRSD without direct support from researchers.[211] Teachers were able to successfully implement SRSD using a practice-based professional development (PBPD) model.[212] This model included many aspects of instruction common to teaching students how to enact SRL, including creating a warm, welcoming climate where teachers acted as collaborators in the implementation, basing the professional development on the strengths and needs of teachers and their students, providing opportunities for teachers to watch, practice, and analyze SRSD in action, and then scaffolding and fading support through feedback as teachers implemented SRSD in their classrooms.

The success of the SRSD model bodes well for scaling up interventions designed to foster positive self-regulation in education. Ultimately, the success of such interventions depends upon not just whether they can be implemented with efficacy but whether they can be scaled to new contexts efficiently. Incorporation of materials and practices on self-regulation in education into educator preparation programs is a powerful way to increase the likelihood that students receive appropriate instruction, but there will always be a need for ongoing, localized support for educators who wish to implement such instruction. The PBPD model, and its success at implementing the SRSD model in context, is one way of promoting self-regulation in education in a cost-effective, scalable manner.

TEACHERS' DUAL ROLES AS SELF-REGULATED LEARNERS AND TEACHERS OF SELF-REGULATED LEARNING

Teachers and other education professionals play critical roles in formal and informal school environments, and they can have pronounced effects upon students' likelihood of effectively engaging self-regulation in education.[213] This volume has focused on students' self-regulation in education, and there are other texts in this series that go into depth regarding teacher beliefs[214] and teacher expectations,[215] as well as other excellent resources detailing comprehensive approaches to educating students to self-regulate in education.[19] Nonetheless, a review of how educators can foster self-regulation in education must also discuss teachers' dual roles as both learners of and teachers of self-regulation in education.

It is difficult for people to teach things they themselves do not understand. Therefore, to be effective instructors of self-regulation in education, teachers must also possess strong capacities and knowledge for self-regulation and SRL.[208,216] In essence, they have a dual role: they must be learners of self-regulation in education as well as teachers of it. For example, teachers often have to acquire new knowledge and skills when preparing to teach a new topic in the curriculum or moving to a new grade level. Doing so requires that teachers themselves can enact effective SRL.

Likewise, self-regulation in education taps teachers' resources (i.e., energy depletion), just as it does for their students. Also like their students, teachers can face challenges within and outside of school that can deplete their self-regulatory resources, making them less likely to successfully self-regulate their own responses or to help their students to do so. Therefore, the success of self-regulation and SRL interventions likely depends to a significant degree on how well teachers can self-regulate while helping others do so as well.

Helping students monitor and control their cognition, motivation, emotion, and behavior requires the ability to teach self-regulation in education. Some teachers are similar to their students in that their own educational career may not have emphasized, or even directly taught, self-regulatory knowledge, skills, or beliefs. Pre-service education programs may be the first time these teachers encounter the idea of self-regulation in education as a desired outcome of formal or informal schooling. Pre-service and in-service teachers who have mastered many aspects of their position (i.e., content knowledge, pedagogical content knowledge) may be challenged by having to learn how to support students' self-regulation as well.[19] Therefore, teachers may have many of the same challenges as their students (i.e., limited resources for self-regulation, lack of explicit instruction in SRL, internal and external self-regulatory demands and pressures). The growing imperative to make self-regulation in education a desired student outcome brings with it the imperative to make it an aspect of teacher education, training, and support as well.[20] Teachers would also benefit from understanding the literature in co-regulation and socially shared regulation of learning, which are important topics beyond the scope of this text.[45]

More research is needed on how best to integrate instruction and support into teacher preparation and professional development programs, but it is clear that teachers should not be asked to teach their students how to self-regulate in education (i.e., adopting the teacher's role) if they have never received such instruction themselves (i.e., the learner's role). On the other hand, more research is needed to determine whether teachers' facility with self-regulation in education is a key predictor of teacher retention and student success, above and beyond other metrics such as IQ and prior preparation. It seems reasonable to suspect that just as self-regulation in education predicts students' learning and performance above and beyond IQ and other factors, it might serve a similar role for teachers and their success.

SUMMARY OF HOW EDUCATORS CAN HELP STUDENTS BECOME BETTER SELF-REGULATORS IN EDUCATION

There is ample empirical evidence that self-regulation and SRL play key roles in students' success in school, both within and outside of the classroom. Thankfully, there is also evidence of effective self-regulation and SRL interventions, which can be implemented successfully by teachers and other adults in education. These interventions share many common elements, such as direct instruction of knowledge and skills, scaffolded and faded support for students' acquisition and practice of those skills, the creation of educational climates where such practice is seen as a valuable and normative aspect of education in general, and provision of ongoing training and support for educators and other adults implementing such interventions.

Self-regulation in education is likely best taught abstractly at first, but then quickly contextualized and practiced in authentic contexts, including both formal (i.e., classrooms) and informal (i.e., lunch rooms, playgrounds) educational settings. To implement self-regulation in education effectively, students must learn things about themselves, about others, and about the various strategies that can be used, including when they should be used. Learning about oneself, and how to address both one's strengths and one's weaknesses, may be easier for older students to do, but younger students can also do this with support. Older students will likely benefit from continued instruction in self-regulation in education because as their contexts, relationships, and goals become more complex, so must their efforts to plan, enact, monitor, and control. Of course, much more research is needed regarding how to most effectively and efficiently develop students' capacity for self-regulation in education, but the basics of this process are clear.

Nonetheless, one aspect of instructing and support self-regulation in education that does not get sufficient attention is diagnosis. Instruction, scaffolding, and fading of support all require that educators be able to accurately assess students' current knowledge, skills, beliefs, and capacity for self-regulation in education.[124] Such diagnosis is not easy or straightforward, nor is it often something that can be done quickly. Recognizing that students are struggling with self-regulation in education is one thing, but it is much more difficult to diagnose exactly which targets, phases, or processes of self-regulation should be the focus on intervention. There are dynamic interactions among these aspects of self-regulation in education and the context surrounding the student, which makes accurate diagnosis even more difficult. Is the student that is currently acting out in class doing so because of ego depletion, a lack of strategy knowledge for self-regulation, or insufficient understanding of the value in doing so? When students struggle with homework, is it because of a lack of sufficient background knowledge, the use of inefficient strategies, or some aspects of home-life preventing sufficient time to do the work? There are myriad possibilities as to why students may not be succeeding in school, and more research is needed on how to help educators diagnosis student performance and then determine how to tailor instruction and support accordingly.

Five

What Is the Future of Self-Regulation in Education?

Successful students must be adept at enacting self-regulation in education. Scholarly literatures can be divided into silos such as SRL research or self-regulation research, but students, and their experiences in formal and informal educational environments, cannot. Students have to balance the pursuit of academic goals, such as the mastery of content and getting good grades, with a myriad of well-being goals involving their physical and mental health, conceptions of themselves, and relations with others. Self-regulating in ways to achieve these goals can be challenging because people have a limited, common pool of resources, and acts of self-regulation in education deplete this pool. When the pool is empty, self-regulation in education of any sort becomes much more challenging and far less likely to occur. With rest and support, the pool of resources can be replenished, but it is better still to avoid depleting the pool at all. The better students become at effectively self-regulating in education, the less often they have to do so, and the more resources they have available for when they do.

When self-regulation in education is needed, it involves active planning, enacting, monitoring, controlling, and reflecting upon a number of internal (e.g., cognition, motivation, affect) and external (e.g., teachers, friends, environment) factors that can occur before, during, and after learning. Students adept at self-regulation in education make conscious decisions about how to inhibit maladaptive cognition, emotions, and behaviors, and replace them with more adaptive ones. Likewise, they rely on efficient and effective strategies for achieving their goals, and they attend to reliable intuitions and experiences regarding that progress, adjusting their plans and actions as needed. Such active, thoughtful self-regulation in education relies on a number of core cognitive processes called "executive functions," whose influence upon performance decreases over time as students develop and learn effective ways of managing the pursuit of their goals. Students' developmental trajectory for self-regulation in education is the result of a dynamic interaction of biological, environmental, and self-generated factors, which thankfully is amenable to intervention by others and, with time and instruction, the students themselves. Even the most adept student will struggle to self-regulate in challenging educational situations, and likewise even the students least likely to self-regulate can do so with proper support. Self-regulation in education is not something students can or cannot do but rather something that is more or less likely to occur based upon interactions between people and contexts. Educators are in the privileged position to directly intervene with students to increase their capability for self-regulating in education, as well as create environments where such interventions are less likely to be needed.

Careful review of the literatures comprising SRL and self-regulation reveals how students' ability and likelihood of enacting self-regulation in education is a powerful predictor of success, both in academics and in life, above and beyond the influence of factors less in students' control, such as IQ or family wealth. Self-regulation in education is not a panacea, nor is it the only way to address educational inequities. But self-regulation in education is worthy of being an explicit goal of education, and an aspect of educator and researcher preparation. Much has been discovered about the role of self-regulation in education, and yet there is much more to be known. The future of self-regulation in education research and practice requires thoughtful partnerships between educators and researchers to understand how to help students succeed generally, across academic disciplines, and within changing and increasingly salient contexts such as learning with technology and in collaboration.

Acknowledging the work to be done to better understand the practice and research of self-regulation in education does not diminish the lessons learned on how to help students be more effective self-regulators. Educators can do much to instruct and support self-regulation in education, ranging from direct instruction with explicit explanations of how to self-regulate in education more effectively to indirect but no less essential efforts to create environments where students feel comfortable and confident pushing themselves to acquire these important, yet challenging, sets of knowledge, skills, and beliefs. Nonetheless, every individual student's experience is unique, requiring educators who can combine best practices with artful understanding of students' needs. Teachers were once students too, and the degree to which they did or did not learn to self-regulate in education will directly inform how well they can help their students do so. Therefore, just as there is need to make self-regulation in education a specific, valued outcome for students, it must also be a valued outcome in educator preparation programs (see Table 5.1).

In sum, the literatures in SRL and self-regulation have been integrated in this text on self-regulation in education. Viewing self-regulation in education as a holistic phenomenon, comprised of active, thoughtful striving toward a balance of

TABLE 5.1 Some key points about self-regulation in education

- Self-regulation in education requires both self-regulated learning and self-regulation.
- Self-regulation in education predicts academic outcomes, but little is known about how self-regulated learning and self-regulation interact to predict academic performance.
- Ideally, students utilize automatized, effective, and efficient strategies for tasks in education; when such strategies are not known or fail to work, self-regulation in education is needed.
- Students vary in the likelihood they will successfully enact self-regulation in education, with context a strong influence upon this likelihood.
- Self-regulated learning and self-regulation require effort to enact, and both draw from a common pool of resources.
- When self-regulation in education resources are depleted, the likelihood of enacting successful self-regulation in education decreases.
- Educators and other adults should endeavor to create environments where, for all students, self-regulation in education is more likely to be enacted when needed.
- The more students understand themselves, their context, and self-regulation in education, the fewer resources self-regulation in education takes to enact, leaving more resources for learning and other educational activities.
- Effective self-regulation in education interventions utilize direct instruction, scaffolding, fading, and ongoing support for implementers.
- Teachers have dual roles as both learners and teachers of self-regulation in education.

academic and well-being goals, allows for a better understanding of the current literature and students' experience. It also points to a number of directions for future research, whose pursuit should blend the wisdom, resources, and interests of practitioners and scholars.

MEASURING SELF-REGULATION IN EDUCATION

Before educators and other adults can help students more effectively self-regulate in education, they need to assess students' self-regulatory capacity, knowledge, and skills. In the self-regulation literature, there are a number of task-based measures of self-regulation, with one of the most popular being the "marshmallow test."[217] This task involves a researcher putting a marshmallow in front of young children and telling them they can eat it if they wish, but, if they wait to eat it until the researcher returns from a break, they can have two marshmallows. Children's ability to "delay gratification" (i.e., resist eating the marshmallow before the researcher returns) has been shown to predict many desirable outcomes later in life, such as academic and job performance. There are numerous other task-based measures of various aspects of self-regulation (i.e., working memory capacity, ability to inhibit), but most require training to implement and interpret properly. School psychologists are one of the professionals in schools with the training to administer such tests, and, while their results can be helpful for teachers working with these children, often there are not enough school psychologists to assess large numbers of students at any particular time. Further, there are concerns that these tests are inauthentic (i.e., how often are children asked to delay gratification for no apparent reason, by a researcher who is a stranger?) and relatively unaffected by variations in motivation, volition, or metamotivation,[26,47] making them inaccurate measures of what students can actually do. It may be the case that such tests underestimate students' abilities or, even worse, that they are differentially accurate: they may measure certain students' abilities quite well, while doing a poor job with other students (e.g., doing a good job measuring the capabilities of students with high self-efficacy, but doing a poor job with students who have low self-efficacy). Further, there is an ongoing debate as to whether such measures only capture students' ability to self-regulate for a specific task (e.g., resisting the temptation to eat a dessert) or if they actually provide valid information about how students self-regulate in general, across other personal and academic tasks and contexts.[218] More research is needed on how to accurately and fairly measure self-regulation, the degree to which students' ability to self-regulate in one task and context generalizes to other tasks and contexts, and how to create assessments that can be implemented by education professionals beyond those with specialized training (i.e., school psychologists) so that more teachers can get good information about their students' current level of self-regulatory functioning.

Researchers interested in measuring students' SRL have faced similar challenges. Task-based measures of SRL are time-consuming to administer and interpret, and often they are not sufficiently scalable to assist teachers in diagnosis and intervention.[136,219] Many researchers have turned to self-report measures of SRL, which often involve asking students to indicate the degree to which they agree or disagree with statements such as, "When I study for a test, I try to put together the information from class and from the book."[220] Such measures are easy to administer, score, and analyze but have several limitations. First, very young children may not be able to understand the statements sufficiently to respond in accurate ways. Second, many of these measures include statements written at a general level, such as asking how students study for school overall, or for a class overall. It is not clear whether these measures capture discipline-or task-specific aspects of SRL. Third, some researchers have expressed concerns that students are poor reporters of their own SRL, because much of what happens in SRL is tacit.[221] Fourth, researchers continue to debate whether SRL should be conceptualized as an aptitude that is relatively independent of context (i.e., similar to using the marshmallow test to infer about students' ability to self-regulate in other settings and ways) or as a series of events that are dependent upon the learning task and context.[222] Advocates for an event-based conceptualization of SRL have argued that self-report measures are not valid because students respond to them out of the context of actually engaging in SRL.[223] Finally, self-report measures are better measures of domain-general conceptualizations of SRL than domain-specific conceptualizations. Many researchers have questioned whether SRL is primarily a domain-specific or even task-specific phenomenon, which if true would call into question the validity of inferences from self-report measures.[49,50,51]

On the other hand, taking an event-based, domain-specific, or task-specific conceptualization of SRL requires asking students to engage in a learning task and then somehow capturing what they are doing, thinking, and feeling on a moment-to-moment basis. Various event-based measures exist (e.g., microanalysis, think-aloud protocols, computer-based trace data logs), but most are resource-intensive and do not scale well to everyday use in a classroom.[219] Researchers continue to work on more valid, effective, and scalable measures of SRL, and there is promise in the field of learning analytics for using data from computer-based learning environments, games, and learning management systems to make inferences about students' ability to enact SRL.[224,225] This is a burgeoning area of research, proceeding at a rapid pace. The hope is that learning analytics will allow the capture of reliable, accurate data about students' self-regulation, at scale.

SCAFFOLDING SELF-REGULATION IN EDUCATION

In the process of scaffolding students' self-regulation in education, diagnosis is not the only key aspect. While much is known about how to effectively instruct and support students' acquisition of self-regulation and SRL capacity, there is still much to be learned about how to do these things in the most efficient, effective, and comprehensive manner. There are numerous interventions available, but more research is needed regarding which aspects of those interventions are maximally effective and necessary for supporting self-regulation in education, and which aspects are less effective or even unnecessary and thus can be discarded to save time and effort. Some researchers have argued for a focus on the meta-cognitive aspects of self-regulation in education; others, for the cognitive or motivational ones. Volition was a prominent topic in the late twentieth century, but it has received less attention more recently. Social psychology interventions, such as a focus on a growth mindset and mental contrasting and implementation interventions, have shown strong effects[226] that should be tested for replication and generalization. Issues of transfer or generalizability are prominent: to what degree, if at all, does training in self-regulation in education in one context (e.g., a history class) lead to better self-regulation in other contexts (e.g., mathematics or science classes)? Finally, more research is needed regarding how the efficacy of scaffolding varies by the context in which it is provided. The classroom climate and ways in which teachers instruct, assess, and establish rapport with students may interact with different types of scaffolding interventions, making some more effective in some contexts than others.[227]

UNDERSTANDING THE SOCIAL ASPECTS
OF SELF-REGULATION IN EDUCATION

Another exciting area of new scholarship and practice involves conceptualizations of self-regulation in education as a situated, dynamic interaction among people and contexts.[45] Rather than focusing on the "self" part of self-regulation, this conceptualization starts from the perspective that all individual action arises from, and is influenced by, individuals' social and cultural history and the contexts in which they act. Even when alone, people self-regulate in ways they were taught and toward goals that have been influenced by people's social and cultural history. Therefore, even "self" regulation is social. Likewise, it is important to understand how individuals in turn influence others around them. By taking into account the social and cultural history of people and contexts, researchers can adopt new perspectives on self-regulation in education and how it evolves over time. Much of the work in this area has been called socially shared regulation of learning (SSRL).[44,45]

The importance of SSRL is particularly apparent when thinking about students engaged in collaboration. Certainly, individual students who collaborate in a group engage in their own self-regulation. However, true collaboration requires those individuals to also consider and adapt to the groups' social and academic goals, which requires shared regulation.[48] In SSRL collaborations, the group members engage in deliberate shared negotiation of group motivation, goals, strategies, evaluations, and adaptations. As the work is done, group members must collaboratively monitor progress, enact control, and maintain sufficient levels of volition. Throughout collaboration, the social and cultural history of the group members, as well as the unique aspects of the context in which they are doing the work, influence how the group interacts. Importantly, SSRL requires attending to the motivational, volitional, and emotional climate within the group. Ideally, collaborative groups take shared responsibility for maintaining positive relations and regulating their interactions in ways that lead to not only progress toward goals but also to mutual care and group learning. Of course, at times during collaborative learning, particular individuals may have specialized knowledge, skills, or beliefs that would benefit one or more members of the group. In these cases, individuals can engage in co-regulation, where they directly support one or more other members of the group in some aspect of regulation or task completion. The distinctions between self-regulation, co-regulation, and socially shared regulation of learning are important contributions to the literature, particularly when considering how students collaborate and how each student's social and cultural history can influence those collaborations.

The SSRL perspective is certainly relevant when students collaborate, but it can help educators and researchers understand dynamics in any setting where multiple students are present. The ways in which students do and do not share group goals and regulation can be important factors determining individual students' likelihood of enacting self-regulation in education.[228] SSRL, and other situated perspectives on self-regulation, are relatively new areas of scholarship boasting tremendous promise as ways of conceptualizing the importance of history and context on learning in schools. This framework could be particularly powerful for understanding and eventually supporting more productive collaboration among students and better understanding how context and history shape how students interact with one another and how they interact with teachers as well.[45]

CONCLUSION

The field of self-regulation in education, which is itself a loose grouping of literature in education, psychology, and learning sciences, is a large and ever-growing area of scholarship and applications to practice. In this text, numerous avenues for future research and practice have been identified, grounded in an understanding of the evolution of these ideas within and among the literatures. Much more work is needed to better understand how to help students successfully enact self-regulation in education and how to create environments where students can learn and practice the associated knowledge, skills, and emotions. Evidence from the literature on self-regulation in education certainly supports its role as a primary factor in student success, inside and outside of school, warranting further research and implementation.

AUTHOR'S NOTE

Writing this text required the assistance of many people. My thanks to Patricia Alexander, Rebecca Novack, and Daniel Schwartz for selecting me to participate in this series and for their feedback and support throughout the writing of this text. Numerous doctoral students read early drafts of this text, helping me to identify gaps in my thinking and writing, including Elizabeth Allen, Brian Cartiff, Dana Copeland, Nikki Lobczowski, and Christopher Oswald. The two experts who reviewed this text provided invaluable feedback and advice. Finally, I would like to thank my family, Mira Brancu, Jacob Greene, and Avery Greene, for their patience and support. They are the reason I continue to self-regulate in education.

Conditional knowledge: information about the circumstances in which particular knowledge or strategies are helpful or not helpful; often called "when" knowledge

Co-regulation: when one individual supports or assists another individual in terms of self- or shared-regulation of learning

Declarative knowledge: specific information and ideas that are stored in, and retrievable from, long-term memory; often called "what" knowledge

Dosage: a term used in intervention implementation research referring to how often students need to be exposed to an intervention for an effect to occur, or how much of an intervention is necessary to achieve a desired effect

Executive functions: a core set of cognitive processes used when conscious, active attention, enactment, monitoring, and control are necessary to achieve valued goals

Feeling of knowing: a term from metacognition research describing people's judgment of whether they know a particular piece of information, even though they cannot recall it at the moment

Fidelity of implementation: the degree to which a school intervention is implemented as designed

Metacognition: commonly defined as thinking about thinking; also defined as any knowledge or cognitive process whose object is cognition itself; most definitions of meta-cognition divide it into five subcomponents: metacognitive knowledge, metacognitive skill, metacognitive experience, goals, and strategies

Metacognitive experiences: cues about a person's own cognition that arise while engaging in a task

Metacognitive knowledge: beliefs people have about (1) their own cognition or learning ability, (2) goals and tasks, and (3) actions or strategies

Metacognitive skills: processes used in the monitoring and control of cognition

Motivation: an omnibus term for the various factors (i.e., cognitive, behavioral, emotional) that fuel the pursuit of goals

Procedural knowledge: specific skills and practices that are stored in, and retrievable from, long-term memory; often called "how" knowledge

Self-regulated learning: active, thoughtful pursuit of desired learning goals through planning, enacting, monitoring, controlling, and reflecting upon internal (i.e., cognition, metacognition, motivation, behavior, affect) and external factors (i.e., environment) before, during, and after learning

Self-regulation: active planning, enacting, monitoring, control, and evaluation of cognition, affect, motivation, and behavior in the pursuit of valued goals, particularly when encountering impediments to that pursuit; in this text, this term is used to describe the pursuit of goals aside from those related to learning academic material

Self-regulation in education: a broad term for the ways students in educational environments pursue academic and well-being goals by planning, enacting, monitoring, controlling, and reflecting upon internal (i.e., cognition, metacognition, motivation, behavior, affect) and external factors (i.e., environment) during the pursuit of valued goals including, but not limited to, academic and social goals

Socially shared regulation of learning: the ways in which groups of people work together to regulate the group's cognition, motivation, behavior, and emotion in their pursuit of a shared goal or set of goals

Transfer: the productive use of a previously learned mental representation in a new context and/or to solve a new problem

Valence: an aspect of phenomena related to whether they are positive or negative; e.g., emotions have valence, with some having a positive valence (e.g., happiness) and some having a negative valence (e.g., anger)

Volition: an omnibus term used to describe the energy and methods used to maintain pursuit of a desired goal in the face of difficulties and distractions

References

1 National Education Association. (2014). *Preparing 21st century students for a global society: An educators guide to the "Four Cs."* Washington, DC: National Education Association.

2 OECD. (2013). *Trends shaping education 2013.* Paris, France: Author. doi:10.1787/trends_edu-2013-en

3 Mervis, J. (2009). Study questions value of school software for students. *Science, 323*(5919), 1277.

4 World Bank. (2011). *Learning for all: Investing in people's knowledge and skills to promote development: Education sector strategy 2020.* Washington, DC: The World Bank.

5 Bjork, R. A., Dunlosky, J., & Kornell, N. (2013). Self-regulated learning: Beliefs, techniques, and illusions. *Annual Review of Psychology, 64*(1), 417–444.

6 Zimmerman, B. J., & Schunk, D. H. (2011). Self-regulated learning and performance. In B. J. Zimmerman & D. H. Schunk (Eds.). *Handbook of self-regulation of learning and performance* (pp. 1–12). New York: Routledge.

7 Dent, A. L., & Koenka, A. C. (2016). The relation between self-regulated learning and academic achievement across childhood and adolescence: a meta-analysis. *Educational Psychology Review, 28*(3), 425–474.

8 Dignath, C., & Büttner, G. (2008). Components of fostering self-regulated learning among students: A meta-analysis on intervention studies at primary and secondary school level. *Metacognition and Learning, 3*(3), 231–264.

9 National Research Council. (2012). *Education for life and work: Developing transferable knowledge and skills in the 21st century.* Committee on Defining Deeper Learning and 21st Century Skills, J.W. Pellegrino and M.L. Hilton, Editors. Board on Testing and Assessment and Board on Science Education, Division of Behavioral and Social Sciences and Education. Washington, DC: The National Academies Press.

10 National Governors Association Center for Best Practices. (2010). *Common core state standards.* Washington, DC: National Governors Association Center for Best Practices, Council of Chief State School Officers.

11   NGSS Lead States. (2013). *Next generation science standards: For states, by states* (Vol. 1: The standards). Washington, DC: The National Academies Press.

12   White, M. C., & DiBenedetto, M. K. (in press). Self-regulation: An integral part of standards based education. In. D. H. Schunk & J. A. Greene (Eds.). *Handbook of self-regulation of learning and performance* (2nd Ed.). New York: Routledge.

13   Diamond, A. (2013). Executive functions. *Annual Review of Psychology, 64*, 135–168.

14   Hoyle, R. H., & Gallagher, P. (2015). The interplay of personality and self-regulation. In M. Mikulincer, P. R. Shaver, M. L. Cooper, & R. J. Larsen (Eds.). *APA handbook of personality and social psychology, Volume 4: Personality processes and individual differences* (pp. 189–207). Washington, DC: American Psychological Association.

15   Blair, C., & Raver, C. C. (2015). School readiness and self-regulation: A developmental psychobiological approach. *Annual Review of Psychology, 66*, 711–731.

16   Moffitt, T. E., Arseneault, L., Belsky, D., Dickson, N., Hancox, R. J., Harrington, H., . . . Caspi, A. (2011). A gradient of childhood self-control predicts health, wealth, and public safety. PN*AS Proceedings of the National Academy of Sciences of the United States of America, 108*, 2693–2698.

17   Zimmerman, B. J. (2013). From cognitive modeling to self-regulation: A social cognitive career path. *Educational Psychologist, 48*(3), 135–147.

18   Hoyle, R. J., & Dent, A. L. (in press). Developmental trajectories of skills and abilities relevant for self-regulation of learning and performance. In. D. H. Schunk & J. A. Greene (Eds.). *Handbook of self-regulation of learning and performance* (2nd Ed.). New York: Routledge.

19   Butler, D. L., Schnellert, L., & Perry, N. E. (2017). *Developing self-regulating learners.* Toronto: Pearson.

20   Perry, N. E., Hutchinson, L., Yee, N., & Määttä, M. (in press). Advances in understanding young children's self-regulation for learning. In. D. H. Schunk & J. A. Greene (Eds.). *Handbook of self-regulation of learning and performance* (2nd Ed.). New York: Routledge.

21   Zimmerman, B. J., & Schunk, D. H. (2003). *Educational psychology: A century of contributions.* New York: Routledge.

22   Bandura, A. (1986). *Social foundations of thought and action: A social cognitive theory.* Englewood Cliffs, NJ: Prentice Hall.

23   Flavell, J. H. (1979). Metacognition and cognitive monitoring: A new area of cognitive—developmental inquiry. *American Psychologist, 34*(10), 906–911.

24   Winne, P. H. (2001). Self-regulated learning viewed from models of information processing. In B. J. Zimmerman & D. H. Schunk (Eds.).

Self-regulated learning and academic achievement: Theoretical perspectives (pp. 153–189). Mahwah, NJ: Erlbaum.

25 Veenman, M. V. J. (2011). Learning to self-monitor and self-regulate. In R. E. Mayer & P. A. Alexander (Eds.). *Handbook of research on learning and instruction* (pp. 197–218). New York, NY: Routledge.

26 Miele, D. B., & Scholer, A. A. (2016). Self-regulation of motivation. In K. Wentzel & D. B. Miele (Eds.). *Handbook of motivation at school* (2nd Ed.) (pp. 363–384). New York: Routledge.

27 Murphy, K. P., & Alexander, P. A. (2000). A motivated exploration of motivation terminology. *Contemporary Educational Psychology*, 25, 3–53.

28 Wolters, C. A. (2003). Understanding procrastination from a self-regulated learning perspective. *Journal of Educational Psychology*, 95(1), 179–187.

29 Wolters, C., & Benzon, M. (2013). Assessing and predicting college students' use of strategies for the self-regulation of motivation. *Journal of Experimental Education*, 18, 199–221.

30 Bembenutty, H., & Karabenick, S. A. (2004). Inherent association between academic delay of gratification, future time perspective, and self-regulated learning. *Educational Psychology Review*, 16, 35–57.

31 Bembenutty, H., Cleary, T. J., & Kitsantas, A. (2013). *Applications of self-regulated learning across diverse disciplines: A tribute to Barry J. Zimmerman*. Charlotte, NC: Information Age Publishing.

32 Dörrenbächer, L., & Perels, F. (2015). Volition completes the puzzle: Development and evaluation of an integrative trait model of self-regulated learning. *Frontline Learning and Research*, 3(4), 14–36.

33 Oettingen, G., Schrage, J., & Gollwitzer, P. M. (2015). Volition. In L. Corno & E. M. Anderman (Eds.). *Handbook of educational psychology* (pp. 104–118). New York: Routledge.

34 Corno, L. (2001). Volitional aspects of self-regulated learning. In B. J. Zimmerman & D. H. Schunk (Eds.). *Self-regulated learning and academic achievement: Theoretical perspectives* (pp. 191–225). Mahwah, NJ: Erlbaum.

35 Baumeister, R. F., Vohs, K. D., & Tice, D. M. (2007). The strength model of self-control. *Current Directions in Psychological Science*, 16(6), 351–355.

36 Boekaerts, M. (2011). Emotions, emotion regulation, and self-regulation of learning. In B. J. Zimmerman & D. H. Schunk (Eds.). *Handbook of self-regulation of learning and performance* (pp. 408–425). New York, NY: Routledge.

37 Zimmerman, B. (1986). Becoming a self-regulated learner: Which are the key subprocesses? *Contemporary Educational Psychology*, 11, 307–313.

38 Paris, S. G., & Paris, A. H. (2001). Classroom applications of research on self-regulated learning. *Educational Psychologist*, 36(2), 89–101.

39   Schmader, T., Johns, M., & Forbes, C. (2008). An integrated process model of stereotype threat effects on performance. *Psychological Review*, 115(2), 336–356.

40   Duckworth, A. L., Gendler, T. S., & Gross, J. J. (2014). Self-control in school-age children. *Educational Psychologist*, 49(3), 199–217.

41   Kalyuga, S. (2007). Expertise reversal effect and its implications for learner-tailored instruction. *Educational Psychology Review*, 19, 509–539. http://dx.doi.org/10.1007/s10648-007-9054-3

42   Dinsmore, D. L., Alexander, P. A., & Loughlin, S. M. (2008). Focusing the conceptual lens on metacognition, self-regulation, and self-regulated learning. *Educational Psychology Review*, 20, 391–409.

43   Sitzman, T., & Ely, K. (2011). A meta-analysis of self-regulated learning in work-related training and educational attainment: What we know and where we need to go. *Psychological Bulletin*, 137(3), 421–442.

44   Hadwin, A. F., Järvelä, S., & Miller, M. (2011). Self-regulated, co-regulated, and socially shared regulation of learning. In B. J. Zimmerman & D. H. Schunk (Eds.). *Handbook of self-regulation of learning and performance* (pp. 65–84). New York, NY: Routledge.

45   Hadwin, A. F., Järvelä, S., & Miller, M. (in press). Understanding the role of self-regulation, co-regulation and shared regulation in collaborative learning environments. In. D. H. Schunk & J. A. Greene (Eds.). *Handbook of self-regulation of learning and performance* (2nd Ed.). New York: Routledge.

46   Thelen, E. & Smith, L. B. (2006). Dynamic systems theories. In Richard M. Lerner & William Damon (Eds.). *Handbook of child psychology* (pp. 258–312). Hoboken, NJ: Wiley.

47   Zelazo, P. D., Blair, C. B., & Willoughby, M. T. (2016). *Executive function: Implications for education* (NCER 2017–2000). Washington, DC: National Center for Education Research, Institute of Education Sciences, U.S. Department of Education.

48   Järvenoja, H., Järvelä, S., & Malmberg, J. (2015). Understanding the process of motivational, emotional and cognitive regulation in learning situations. *Educational Psychologist*, 50(3), 204–219.

49   Alexander, P. A., Dinsmore, D. L., Parkinson, M. M., & Winters, F. I. (2011). Self-regulated learning in academic domains. In B. Zimmerman & D. Schunk (Eds.). *Handbook of self-regulation of learning and performance* (pp. 393–407). New York: Routledge.

50   Greene, J. A., Bolick, C. M., Jackson, W. P., Caprino, A. M., Oswald, C., & McVea, M. (2015). Domain-specificity of self-regulated learning processing in science and history digital libraries. *Contemporary Educational Psychology*, 42, 111–128.

51 Greene, J. A., Bolick, C. M., Caprino, A. M., Deekens, V. M., McVea, M., Yu, S. B., & Jackson, W. P. (2015). Fostering high-school students' self-regulated learning online and across academic domains. *The High School Journal*, 99(1), 88–106.

52 Pintrich, P. R. (2000). The role of goal orientation in self-regulated learning. In M. Boekaerts, P. Pintrich, & M. Zeidner (Eds.). *Handbook of self-regulation* (pp. 451–502). San Diego, CA: Academic Press.

53 Corno, L., & Mandinach, E. (1983). The role of cognitive engagement in classroom learning and motivation. *Educational Psychologist*, 18, 88–108.

54 Kahneman, D. (2011). *Thinking, fast and slow*. New York: Macmillan.

55 van Merrienboer, J. J. G., & Sweller, J. (2005). Cognitive load theory and complex learning: Recent developments and future directions. *Educational Psychology Review*, 17(2), 147–177.

56 Cleary, T. J., & Zimmerman, B. J. (2004). Self-regulation empowerment program: A school-based program to enhance self-regulated and self-motivated cycles of student learning. *Psychology in the Schools*, 41(5), 537–550.

57 Schunk, D. H., & Greene, J. A. (in press). *Handbook of self-regulation of learning and performance* (2nd Ed.). New York: Routledge.

58 Winne, P. H., & Hadwin, A. F. (2008). The weave of motivation and self-regulated learning. In D. Schunk & B. Zimmerman (Eds.). *Motivation and self-regulated learning: Theory, research, and applications* (pp. 297–314). Mahwah, NJ: Erlbaum.

59 Greene, J. A., & Azevedo, R. (2007). A theoretical review of Winne and Hadwin's model of self-regulated learning: New perspectives and directions. *Review of Educational Research*, 77(3), 334–372.

60 Greene, J. A., Hutchison, L. A., Costa, L., & Crompton, H. (2012). Investigating how college students' task definitions and plans relate to self-regulated learning processing and understanding of a complex science topic. *Contemporary Educational Psychology*, 37, 307–320. http://dx.doi.org/10.1016/j.cedpsych.2012.02.002

61 Pinker, S. (2003). *The blank slate: The modern denial of human nature*. New York: Penguin.

62 VanSledright, B. (2002). Confronting history's interpretive paradox while teaching fifth graders to investigate the past. *American Educational Research Journal*, 39, 1089–1115.

63 Wineburg, S. (1991). On the reading of historical texts: Notes on the breach between school and academy. *American Educational Research Journal*, 28, 495–519.

64 Linnenbrink-Garcia, L., & Patall, E. A. (2016). Motivation. In E. Anderman & L. Corno (Eds.). *Handbook of educational psychology* (3rd Ed., pp. 91–103). New York, NY: Taylor & Francis.

65   Schraw, G. (2006). Knowledge: Structures and processes. In P. Alexander & P. Winne (Eds.). *Handbook of educational psychology* (pp. 245–263). Mahwah, NJ: Erlbaum.

66   Mueller, P. A., & Oppenheimer, D. M. (2014). The pen is mightier than the keyboard: Advantages of longhand over laptop note taking. *Psychological Science*, 25(6), 1159–1168.

67   Dunlosky, J., Rawson, K. A., Marsh, E. J., Nathan, M. J., & Willingham, D. T. (2013). Improving students' learning with effective learning techniques: Promising directions from cognitive and educational psychology. *Psychological Science in the Public Interest*, 14(1), 4–58.

68   Weiner, B. (2010). The development of an attribution-based theory of motivation: A history of ideas. *Educational Psychologist*, 45(1), 28–36.

69   Dweck, C. S. (2006). *Mindset*. New York, NY: Random House.

70   Tauber, S., & Dunlosky, J. (2016). A brief history of metamemory research and handbook overview. In J. Dunlosky & S. K. Tauber (Eds.). *The Oxford handbook of metamemory* (pp. 7–21). Oxford, UK: Oxford University Press.

71   Maehr, M. L., & Zusho, A. (2009). Achievement goal theory: The past, present, and future. In K. Wentzel & A. Wigfield (Eds.). *Handbook of motivation at school* (pp. 76–104). New York, NY: Routledge.

72   Zimmerman, B. (2000). Attaining self-regulation: A social cognitive perspective. In M. Boekaerts, P. Pintrich, & M. Zeidner (Eds.). *Handbook of self-regulation* (pp. 13–39). San Diego, CA: Academic Press.

73   Immordino-Yang, M. H., & Damasio, A. (2007). We feel, therefore we learn: The relevance of affective and social neuroscience to education. *Mind, Brain, and Education*, 1, 3–10.

74   Boekaerts, M., & Pekrun, R. (2015). Emotions and emotion regulation in academic settings. In L. Corno & E. M. Anderman (Eds.). *Handbook of educational psychology* (pp. 76–90). New York: Routledge.

75   Efklides, A. (2011). Interactions of metacognition with motivation and affect in self-regulated learning: The MASRL model. *Educational Psychologist*, 46(1), 6–25.

76   Eisenberg, N., Valiente, C., & Eggum, N. D. (2010). Self-regulation and school readiness. *Early Education and Development*, 21(5), 681–698.

77   Karabenick, S. A., & Gonida, E. N. (in press). Academic help seeking as a self-regulated learning strategy. In. D. H. Schunk & J. A. Greene (Eds.). *Handbook of self-regulation of learning and performance* (2nd Ed.). New York: Routledge.

78   Nelson-Le Gall, S. (1981). Help-seeking: An understudied problem-solving skill in children. *Developmental Review*, 1, 224–246.

79   Wentzel, K. R., & Ramani, G. (Eds.) (2016). *Handbook of social influences in school contexts: social-emotional, motivation, and cognitive outcomes*. New York: Routledge.

80   Dweck, C. S., & Master, A. (2008). Self-theories motivate self-regulated learning. In D. H. Schunk & B. J. Zimmerman (Eds.). *Motivation and self-regulated learning: Theory, research, and applications* (pp. 31–51). New York, NY: Lawrence Erlbaum Associates.

81   Yeager, D. S., & Dweck, C. S. (2012). Mindsets that promote resilience: When students believe that personal characteristics can be developed. *Educational Psychologist, 47*, 302–314.

82   Burnette, J. L., O'Boyle, E. H., VanEpps, E. M., Pollack, J. M., & Finkel, E. J. (2013). Mind-sets matter: A meta-analytic review of implicit theories and self-regulation. *Psychological Bulletin, 139*(3), 655–701.

83   Blackwell, L., Trzesniewski, K., & Dweck, C. (2007). Implicit theories of intelligence predict achievement across an adolescent transition: A longitudinal study and an intervention. *Child Development, 78*(1), 246–263.

84   Greene, J. A., Costa, L. C., Robertson, J., Pan, Y., & Deekens, V. (2010). Exploring relations among college students' prior knowledge, implicit theories of intelligence, and self-regulated learning in a hypermedia environment. *Computers & Education, 55*, 1027–1043. doi:10.1016/j.compedu.2010.04.013

85   Zimmerman, B. J. (2008). Investigating self-regulation and motivation: Historical background, methodological developments, and future prospects. *American Educational Research Journal, 45*(1), 166–183.

86   Efklides, A. (2012). Commentary: How readily can findings from basic cognitive psychology research be applied in the classroom? *Learning and Instruction, 22*, 290–295.

87   Alexander, P. A. (2014). Thinking critically and analytically about critical-analytic thinking: An introduction. *Educational Psychology Review, 26*, 469–476.

88   Greene, J. A., & Yu, S. B. (2016). Educating critical thinkers: The role of epistemic cognition. *Policy Insights from the Behavioral and Brain Sciences, 3*(1), 45–53.

89   Chinn, C. A., Buckland, L. A., & Samarapungavan, A. (2011). Expanding the dimensions of epistemic cognition: Arguments from philosophy and psychology. *Educational Psychologist, 46*, 141–167.

90   Corno, L. (2011). Studying self-regulation habits. In B. J. Zimmerman & D. H. Schunk (Eds.). *Handbook of self-regulation of learning and performance* (pp. 361–375). New York, NY: Routledge.

91   Schraw, G., Wadkins, T., & Olafson, L. (2007). Doing the things we do: A grounded theory of academic procrastination. *Journal of Educational Psychology, 99*(1), 12.

92   Job, V., Walton, G. M., Bernecker, K., & Dweck, C. S. (2015). Implicit theories about willpower predict self-regulation and grades in everyday life. *Journal of Personality and Social Psychology, 108*(4), 637–647.

93   Maier, S. F., & Seligman, M. E. (2016). Learned helplessness at fifty: Insights from neuroscience. *Psychological Review*, 123(4), 349.

94   Rutherford, T. (2017). The measurement of calibration in real contexts. *Learning and Instruction*, 47, 33–42.

95   Alexander, P. A. (2013). Calibration: What is it and why it matters? An introduction to the special issue on calibrating calibration. *Learning and Instruction*, 24, 1–3.

96   Dunlosky, J., & Thiede, K. W. (2013). Four cornerstones of calibration research: Why understanding students' judgments can improve their achievement. *Learning and Instruction*, 24, 58–61.

97   DiFrancesca, D., Nietfeld, J. L., & Cao, L. (2016). A comparison of high and low achieving students on self-regulated learning variables. *Learning and Individual Differences*, 45, 228–236.

98   Finn, B., & Tauber, S. K. (2015). When confidence is not a signal of knowing: How students' experiences and beliefs about processing fluency can lead to miscalibrated confidence. *Educational Psychology Review*, 27, 567–586.

99   Winne, P. H. (2017). Leveraging big data to help each learner upgrade learning and accelerate learning science. *Teachers College Record*, 119(3). http://www.tcrecord.org/Content.asp?ContentId=21769.

100   Reid, A. J., Morrison, G. R., & Bol, L. (2016). Knowing what you know: Improving metacomprehension and calibration accuracy in digital text. *Educational Technology Research and Development*, 65(1), 1–17.

101   Thiede, K. W., & Bruin, A. de. (in press). Self-regulated learning of comprehension processes. In. D. H. Schunk & J. A. Greene (Eds.). *Handbook of self-regulation of learning and performance* (2nd Ed.). New York: Routledge.

102   Murray, D. W., Rosanbalm, K., Christopoulos, C., & Hamoudi, A. (2015). *Self-regulation and toxic stress: Foundations for understanding self-regulation from an applied developmental perspective: OPRE report #2015–21*. Washington, DC: Office of Planning, Research and Evaluation, Administration for Children and Families, U.S. Department of Health and Human Services.

103   Serpell, Z. N., & Esposito, A. G. (2016). Development of executive functions: Implications for educational policy and practice. *Policy Insights from the Behavioral and Brain Sciences*, 3(2), 203–210.

104   Baggetta, P., & Alexander, P. A. (2016). Conceptualization and operationalization of executive function. *Mind, Brain, & Education*, 10(1), 10–33.

105   Berger, A. (2011). *Self-regulation: Brain, cognition, and development*. Washington, DC: American Psychological Association.

106   Melby-Lervåg, M., Redick, T. S., & Hulme, C. (2016). Working memory training does not improve performance on measures of intelligence or

other measures of "far transfer": Evidence from a meta-analytic review. *Perspectives on Psychological Science*, 11(4), 512–534.

107 Valiente, C., Lemery-Chalfant, K., & Swanson, J. (2010). Prediction of kindergartners' academic achievement from their effortful control and emotionality: Evidence for direct and moderated relations. *Journal of Educational Psychology*, 102(3), 550–560.

108 Haggar, M. S., & Chatzisarantis, N. L. D. (2016). A multilab preregistered replication of the ego-depletion effect. *Perspectives on Psychological Science*, 11(4), 546–573.

109 Hagger, M. S., Wood, C., Stiff, C., & Chatzisarantis, N. L. D. (2010). Ego depletion and the strength model of self-control: A meta-analysis. *Psychological Bulletin*, 136, 495–525.

110 Duckworth, A. L., Peterson, C., Matthews, M. D., & Kelly, D. R. (2007). Grit: Perseverance and passion for long-term goals. *Journal of Personality and Social Psychology*, 92, 1087–1101. http://dx.doi.org/10.1037/0022-3514.92.6.1087

111 Muenks, K., Wigfield, A., Yang, J. S., & O'Neal, C. R. (2016, December 5). How true is grit? Assessing its relations to high school and college students' personality characteristics, self-regulation, engagement, and achievement. *Journal of Educational Psychology*. Advance online publication. http://dx.doi.org/10.1037/edu0000153

112 Cadima, J., Verschueren, K., Leal, T., & Guedes, C. (2016). Classroom interactions, dyadic teacher—child relationships, and self—regulation in socially disadvantaged young children. *Journal of Abnormal Child Psychology*, 44(1), 7–17.

113 Willoughby, M. T., Wirth, R. J., & Blair, C. B., & The Family Life Project Investigators. (2012). Executive function in early childhood: Longitudinal measurement invariance and developmental change. *Psychological Assessment*, 24, 418–431.

114 Ericsson, K. A., Krampe, R. T., & Tesch-Romer, C. (1993). The role of practice in the acquisition of expert performance. *Psychological Review*, 100, 363–406.

115 Ericsson, K. A., & Pool, R. (2016). *Peak: Secrets from the new science of expertise*. New York: Houghton Mifflin Harcourt Publishing Company.

116 Duckworth, A. L., White, R. E., Matteucci, A. J., Shearer, A., & Gross, J. (2016). A stitch in time: Strategic self-control in high school and college students. *Journal of Educational Psychology*, 108(3), 329–341.

117 Goldman, S. R., Britt, M. A., Brown, W., Cribb, G., George, M., Greenleaf, C., Lee, C. D., Shanahan, C., & Project READI. (2016). Disciplinary literacies and learning to read for understanding: A conceptual framework for disciplinary literacy. *Educational Psychologist*, 51(2), 1–28.

118   Azevedo, R. (2005). Computer environments as metacognitive tools for enhancing learning. *Educational Psychologist*, 40, 193–197.

119   Moos, D. C. (in press). Emerging classroom technology: Using self-regulation principles as a guide for effective implementation. In. D. H. Schunk & J. A. Greene (Eds.). *Handbook of self-regulation of learning and performance* (2nd Ed.). New York: Routledge.

120   Murphy, P. K., Wilkinson, I. A. G., Soter, A. O., Hennessey, M. N., & Alexander, J. F. (2009). Examining the effects of classroom discussion on students' high-level comprehension of text: A meta-analysis. *Journal of Educational Psychology*, 101, 740–764.

121   Murphy, P. K. (in prep). *Classroom discourse in education*. New York: Routledge.

122   de Boer, H., Donker, A. S., & van der Werf, M. P. C. (2014). Effects of the attributes of educational interventins on students' academic performance: A meta-analysis. *Review of Educational Research*, 84(4), 509–545.

123   Kistner, S., Rakoczy, K., Otto, B., Dignath-van Ewijk, C., Büttner, G., & Klieme, E. (2010). Promotion of self-regulated learning in classrooms: Investigating frequency, quality, and consequences for student performance. *Metacognition and Learning*, 5(2), 157–171.

124   van de Pol, J., Volman, M., & Beishuzien, J. (2010). Scaffolding in teacher-student interaction: A decade of research. *Educational Psychology Review*, 22, 271–296.

125   Greene, J. A. (2015). Serious challenges require serious scholarship: Integrating implementation science into the scholarly discourse. *Contemporary Educational Psychology*, 40, 112–120.

126   Murphy, P. K. (2015). Marking the way: School-based interventions that "work." *Contemporary Educational Psychology*, 40, 1–4.

127   Slavin, R. E. (2011). Instruction based on cooperative learning. In R. E. Mayer & P. A. Alexander (Eds.). *Handbook of research on learning and instruction* (pp. 344–360). New York: Routledge.

128   Murphy, P. K., Firetto, C. M., Wei, L., Li, M., & Croninger, R. M. V. (2016). What REALLY works: Optimizing classroom discussions to promote comprehension and critical-analytic thinking. *Policy Insights from the Behavioral and Brain Sciences*, 3, 27–35.

129   Richardson, M., Abraham, C., & Bond, R. (2012). Psychological correlates of university students' academic performance: A systematic review and meta-analysis. *Psychological Bulletin*, 138(2), 353–387. doi:10.1037/a0026838

130   Vernon-Feagans, L., Willougby, M., Garrett-Peters, P., & The Family Life Project Key Investigators. (2016). Predictors of behavioral regulation in

kindergarten: Household chaos, parenting, and early executive functions. *Developmental Psychology*, 52(3), 430–441.

131   Murray, D. W., Rosanbalm, K., & Christopoulos, C. (2016). *Selfregulation and toxic stress report 3: A comprehensive review of selfregulation interventions from birth through young adulthood: OPRE report # 201634.* Washington, DC: Office of Planning, Research and Evaluation, Administration for Children and Families, U.S. Department of Health and Human Services.

132   Diamond, A., & Lee, K. (2011). Interventions shown to aid executive function development in children 4 to 12 years old. *Science*, 333, 959–964.

133   Ryan, R. M., & Deci, E. L. (2016). Facilitating and hindering motivation, learning, and well-being in schools: Research and observations from self-determination theory. In K. R. Wentzel & D. B. Miele (Eds.). *Handbook of motivation at schools* (2nd Ed., pp. 96–119). New York: Routledge.

134   Mayer, R. E. (2004). Should there be a three-strikes rule against pure discovery learning? *American Psychologist*, 59, 14–19.

135   Harkin, B., Webb, T. L., Chang, B. P. I., Prestwich, A., Conner, M., Kellar, I., Benn, Y., & Sheeran, P. (2016). Does monitoring goal progress promote goal attainment? A meta-analysis of the experimental evidence. *Psychological Bulletin*, 142(2), 198–229.

136   Greene, J. A., Yu, S., & Copeland, D. Z. (2014). Measuring critical components of digital literacy and their relationships with learning. *Computers & Education*, 76, 55–69.

137   Alexander, P. A. (1995). Superimposing a situation-specific and domain-specific perspective on an account of self-regulated learning. *Educational Psychologist*, 30(4), 189–193.

138   Wolters, C., Yu, S., & Pintrich, P. (1996). The relation between goal orientation and students' motivational beliefs and self-regulated learning. *Learning and Individual Differences*, 8, 211–238.

139   Mevarech, Z., Verschaffel, L., & de Corte, E. (in press). Metacognitive pedagogies in mathematics classrooms: From kindergarten to college and beyond. In. D. H. Schunk & J. A. Greene (Eds.). *Handbook of self-regulation of learning and performance* (2nd Ed.). New York: Routledge.

140   Roebers, C. M., Cimeli, P., Roethlisberger, M., & Neuenschwander, R. (2012). Executive functioning, metacognition, and self-perceived competence in elementary school children: An explorative study on their interrelations and their role for school achievement. *Metacognition and Learning*, 7, 151–173.

ner). Have technology and multitasking
...erican Educator, 34(2), 23–28.
...riables, in-class laptop multitasking and
...nalysis. Computers & Education, 81, 82–88.
...ay, K. (2015). Aim, shoot, deplete: Play-
regulatory resources. International Journal of
..., 451–456.
.... (2016). Ego depletion increases regula-
...tal media environments. Computers in Human

...010). Ego depletion effects on mathemat-
...chool students: Why take the hard road?
...–281.
...ssey, J. D., & Doolittle, P. E. (2014). Unregu-
...n large lecture classes. Computers & Education,

...(2015). Engaging or distracting: Children's
...tion. Journal of Educational Technology & Society,

...013). E-textbooks at what cost? Performance
...ts. Computers & Education, 72, 18–23.
...iengelkamp, C. (2015). Self-regulation in
...ironments: Effects of learner characteris-
... In Wolfgang Schnotz, Alexander Kauertz,
...iller, & Johanna Pretsch (Eds.). Multidisci-
...rning (pp. 44–67). London: Palgrave Mac-

... Costich, C. M. (2008). Self-regulation of
...sed learning environments: A critical analy-
...20, 429–444.
...& Hoffmann, K. F. (2014). Self-regulation
...ased learning environment. Journal of Educa-

...5). Motivation matters: Interactions between
...caffolding for self-regulated learning within
...Computers in Human Behavior, 52, 338–348.
...et, F., & Khosravifar, B. (2014). Can the use
...ve self-regulated learning strategies be pre-
...prior knowledge in hypermedia-learning
...man Behavior, 39, 356–367.

141   Perels, F., Gürtler, T., & Schmitz, B. (2005). Training of self-regulatory and problem-solving competence. Learning and Instruction, 15, 123–139.

142   Pape, S. J., Bell, C. V., & Yetkin-Ozdemir, I. E. (2013). Sequencing components of mathematics lessons to maximize development of self-regulation: Theory, practice, and intervention. In H. Bembenutty, T. J. Cleary, & A. Kitsantas (Eds.). Applications of self-regulated learning across diverse disciplines: A tribute to Barry J. Zimmerman (pp. 29–58). Charlotte, NC: Information Age Publishing.

143   de Bruin, A. B., & van Gog, T. (2012). Improving self-monitoring and self-regulation: From cognitive psychology to the classroom. Learning and Instruction, 22(4), 245–252.

144   Thiede, K. W., Anderson, M. C. M., & Therriault, D. (2003). Accuracy of metacognitive monitoring affects learning of texts. Journal of Educational Psychology, 95, 66–73.

145   Binbasaran Tüysüzog?lu, B., & Greene, J. A. (2015). An investigation of the role of contingent metacognitive behavior in self-regulated learning. Metacognition & Learning, 10, 77–98. http://dx.doi.org/10.1007/s11409-014-9126-y

146   Guthrie, J. T., Wigfield, A., Barbosa, P., Perencevich, K. C., Taboada, A., Davis, M. H., Scafiddi, N. T., & Tonks, S. (2004). Increasing reading comprehension and engagement through concept-oriented reading instruction. Journal of Educational Psychology, 96, 403–423.

147   Shiu, L., & Chen, Q. (2013). Self and external monitoring of reading comprehension. Journal of Educational Psychology, 105, 78–88.

148   Fernandez, J., & Jamet, E. (2016). Extending the testing effect to self-regulated learning. Metacognition & Learning, 1–26.

149   Graham, S., & Harris, K. (1997). Self-regulation and writing: Where do we go from here? Contemporary Educational Psychology, 22, 102–114.

150   Zimmerman, B., & Reisemberg, R. (1997). Becoming a self-regulated writer: A social cognitive perspective. Contemporary Educational Psychology, 22, 73–101.

151   Graham, S., Harris, K. R., & Olinghouse, N. (in press). Writing and self-regulation. In. D. H. Schunk & J. A. Greene (Eds.). Handbook of self-regulation of learning and performance (2nd Ed.). New York: Routledge.

152   Santangelo, T., Harris, K. R., & Graham, S. (2016). Self-regulation and writing: An overview and meta-analysis. In C. MacArthur, S. Graham, & J. Fitzgerald (Eds.). Handbook of writing research (Vol. 2, pp. 174–193). New York: Guilford.

153   Azevedo, R., Cromley, J. G., Moos, D. C., Greene, J. A., & Winters, F. I. (2011). Adaptive content and process scaffolding: A key to facilitating

students' self-regulated learning with hypermedia. *Instructional Science*, 53(1), 106–140.

154 Sinatra, G. M., & Taasoobshirazi, G. (in press). The self-regulation of learning and conceptual change in science: Research, theory, and educational applications. In. D. H. Schunk & J. A. Greene (Eds.). *Handbook of self-regulation of learning and performance* (2nd Ed.). New York: Routledge.

155 Tippett, C. D. (2010). Refutation text in science education: A review of two decades of research. *International Journal of Science and Mathematics Education*, 8(6), 951–970.

156 Zohar, A., & Barzilai, S. (2013). A review of research on metacognition in science education: Current and future directions. *Studies in Science Education*, 49, 121–169.

157 Hsu, Y.-S., Yen, M.-H., Chang, W.-H., Wang, C.-Y., & Chen, S. (2016). Content analysis of 1998–2012 empirical studies in science reading using a self-regulated learning lens. *International Journal of Science and Mathematics Education*, 14(1), 1–27.

158 Sandoval, W. A. (2016). Disciplinary insights into the study of epistemic cognition. In J. A. Greene, W. A. Sandoval, & I. Bråten (Eds.). *Handbook of epistemic cognition* (pp. 184–194). New York: Routledge.

159 Sinatra, G. M., Kienhues, D., & Hofer, B. K. (2014). Addressing challenges to public understanding of science: Epistemic cognition, motivated reasoning, and conceptual change. *Educational Psychologist*, 49, 123–138.

160 Cleary, T. J., Platten, P., & Nelson, A. C. (2008). Effectiveness of self-regulation empowerment program with urban high school students. *Journal of Advanced Academics*, 20, 70–107.

161 Eilam, B., & Reiter, S. (2014). Long-term self-regulation of biology learning using standard junior high school science curriculum. *Science Education*, 98(4), 705–737.

162 Greene, J. A., Bolick, C. M., & Robertson, J. (2010). Fostering historical knowledge and thinking skills using hypermedia learning environments: The role of self-regulated learning. *Computers & Education*, 54, 230–243.

163 Poitras, E. G., & Lajoie, S. P. (2013). A domain-specific account of self-regulated learning: The cognitive and metacognitive activities involved in learning through historical inquiry. *Metacognition & Learning*, 8, 213–234.

164 Poitras, E. G., & Lajoie, S. P. (2014). Developing an agent-based adaptive system for scaffolding self-regulated learning in history education. *Educational Technology Research and Development*, 62(3), 335–366.

165 Lawless, K. A. (2016). Educational technology: False profit or sacrificial lamb? A review of policy, research, and practice. *Policy Insights from the Behavioral and Brain Sciences*, 3(2), 169–176.

178 Willingham, D. T. (201 rewired how students l

179 Zhang, W. (2014). Lea academic performance:

180 Harma, M., Aktan, T., & ing video games deple *Human-Computer Interaction*.

181 Vanco, B. M., & Christen tory success in education *Behavior*, 62, 602–612.

182 Price, D. A., & Yates, G. C ics performance in prim *Educational Psychology*, 30(3

183 Ragan, E. D., Jennings, S. lated use of laptops over 78, 78–86.

184 McEwen, R. N., & Dube, tablet computer use in 18(4), 9–23.

185 Daniel, D. B., & Woody, W and use of electronic v. pri

186 Mihalca, L., Schnotz, W., computer-based learning tics and instructional sup Heidrun Ludwig, Andrea *plinary Research on Teaching an* millan UK.

187 Winters, F. I., Greene, J. A learning within computer sis. *Educational Psychology Revi*

188 Nietfeld, J. L., Shores, L. F and gender within a gam *tional Psychology*, 106, 961–9

189 Duffy, M., & Azevedo, R. (2 achievement goals and ager an intelligent tutoring syste

190 Taub, M., Azevedo, R., Bou of cognitive and metacogn dicted by learners' levels environments? *Computers in*

191 Biswas, G., Segedy, J. R., & Kinnebrew, J. S. (2013). Smart open-ended learning environments that support learners' cognitive and metacognitive processes. In A. Holzinger & G. Pasi (Eds.). *Human-computer interaction and knowledge discovery in complex, unstructured, big data: Lecture notes in computer science* (Vol. 7947, pp. 303–310). Berlin, Germany: Springer.

192 Pilegard, C., & Fiorella, L. (2016). Helping students help themselves: Generative learning strategies improve middle school students' self-regulation in a cognitive tutor. *Computers in Human Behavior, 65*, 121–126.

193 Bernacki, M. L. (in press). Examining the cyclical, loosely sequenced, and contingent features of self-regulated learning: Trace data and their analysis. In D. H. Schunk & J. A. Greene (Eds.). *Handbook of self-regulation of learning and performance* (2nd Ed.). New York: Routledge.

194 Johnson, A. M., Azevedo, R., & D'Mello, S. K. (2011). The temporal and dynamic nature of self-regulatory processes during independent and externally assisted hypermedia learning. *Cognition and Instruction, 29*, 471–504.

195 Azevedo, R., Harley, J., Trevors, G., Duffy, M., Feyzi-Behnagh, R., Bouchet, F., & Landis, R. S. (2013). Using trace data to examine the complex roles of cognitive, metacognitive, and emotional self-regulatory processes during learning with multi-agent systems. In R. Azevedo & V. Aleven (Eds.). *International handbook of metacognition and learning technologies* (pp. 427–449). Amsterdam, the Netherlands: Springer.

196 D'Mello, S. K., & Graesser, A. C. (2012). AutoTutor and affective AutoTutor: Learning by talking with cognitively and emotionally intelligent computers that talk back. *ACM Transactions on Interactive Intelligent Systems, 2*, 23–39.

197 Jacob, R., & Parkinson, J. (2015). The potential for school-based interventions that target executive function to improve academic achievement: A review. *Review of Educational Research, 85*(4), 512–552.

198 Schwaighofer, M., Fischer, F., & Bühner, M. (2015). Does working memory training transfer? A meta-analysis including training conditions as moderators. *Educational Psychologist, 50*(2), 138–166.

199 Duckworth, A. L., & Allred, K. M. (2012). Temperament in the classroom. In R. L. Shiner & M. Zentner (Eds.). *Handbook of temperament* (pp. 627–644). New York, NY: Guilford Press.

200 Durlak, J. A., Weissberg, R. P., Dymnicki, A. B., Taylor, R. D., & Schellinger, K. (2011). The impact of enhancing students' social and emotional learning: A meta-analysis of school-based universal interventions. *Child Development, 82*, 405–432.

201 Duckworth, A. L., & Carlson, S. M. (2013). Self-regulation and school success. In F. M. E. Grouzet, U. Muller, & B. W. Sokol (Eds.). *Self-regulation*

and autonomy: *Social and developmental dimensions of human conduct* (pp. 208–230). New York, NY: Cambridge University Press.

202   Bierman, K. L., Coie, J. D., Dodge, K. A., Greenberg, M. T., Lochman, J. E., McMahon, R. J., & Pinderhughes, E. (2010). The effects of a multiyear universal social-emotional learning program: The role of student and school characteristics. *Journal of Consulting and Clinical Psychology, 78*, 156–168.

203   Hamre, B. K., & Pianta, R. C. (2005). Can instructional and emotional support in the first-grade classroom make a difference for children at risk of school failure? *Child Development, 76*, 949–967.

204   Gollwitzer, P. M., & Sheeran, P. (2006). Implementation intentions and goal achievement: A meta-analysis of effects and processes. *Advances in Experimental Social Psychology, 38*, 69–119.

205   Duckworth, A. L., Grant, H., Loew, B., Oettingen, G., & Gollwitzer, P. M. (2011). Self-regulation strategies improve self-discipline in adolescents: Benefits of mental contrasting and implementation intentions. *Educational Psychology: An International Journal of Experimental Educational Psychology, 31*(1), 17–26.

206   Zepeda, C. D., Richey, J. E., Ronevich, P., & Nokes-Malach, T. J. (2015). Direct instruction of metacognition benefits adolescent science learning, transfer, and motivation: An in vivo study. *Journal of Educational Psychology, 107*(4), 954.

207   Veenman, M. V. J., Van Hout-Wolters, B. H. A. M., & Afflerbach, P. (2006). Metacognition and learning: Conceptual and methodological considerations. *Metacognition and Learning, 1*, 3–14.

208   Kramarski, B. (in press). Teachers as agents in promoting students' SRL: Research and implications. In D. H. Schunk & J. A. Greene (Eds.). *Handbook of self-regulation of learning and performance* (2nd Ed.). New York: Routledge.

209   Graham, S., McKeown, D., Kiuhara, S., & Harris, K. (2012). A meta-analysis of writing instruction for students in the elementary grades. *Journal of Educational Psychology, 104*, 879–896.

210   Graham, S., Harris, K. R., & McKeown, D. (2013). The writing of students with LD and a meta-analysis of SRSD writing intervention studies: Redux. In L. Swanson, K. R. Harris, & S. Graham (Eds.). *Handbook of learning disabilities* (2nd Ed., pp. 405–438). New York: Guilford Press.

211   Festas, I., Oliveira, A. L., Rebelo, J. A., Damião, M. H., Harris, K., & Graham, S. (2015). Professional development in self-regulated strategy development: Effects on the writing performance of eighth grade Portuguese students. *Contemporary Educational Psychology, 40*, 17–27.

212   Grossman, P., & McDonald, M. (2008). Back to the future: Directions for research in teaching and teacher education. *American Educational Research Journal, 45*, 184–205.

213 Perry, N. E., Hutchinson, L., & Thauberger, C. (2008). Talking about teaching self-regulated learning: Scaffolding student teachers' development and use of practices that promote self-regulated learning. *International Journal of Educational Research*, 47(2), 97–108.

214 Fives, H. (in prep). *Teacher beliefs in education*. New York: Routledge.

215 Rubie-Davies, C. (in prep). *Teacher expectations in education*. New York: Routledge.

216 Kohen, Z., & Kramarski, B. (in press). Promoting mathematics teachers' pedagogical metacognition: A theoretical-practical model and case study. In J. Dori, Z. Mevarech, & D. Baker (Eds.). *Cognition, metacognition, and culture in STEM education*. New York: Springer.

217 Mischel, W. (2014). *The marshmallow test: Mastering self-control*. New York, NY: Little, Brown and Company.

218 Tsukayama, E., Duckworth, A. L., & Kim, B. E. (2013). Domain-specific impulsivity in school-age children. *Developmental Science*, 16, 879–893.

219 Greene, J. A., Dellinger, K., Binbasaran Tuysuzoglu, B., & Costa, L. (2013). A two-tiered approach to analyzing self-regulated learning process data to inform the design of hypermedia learning environments. In R. Azevedo & V. Aleven (Eds.). *International handbook of metacognition and learning technologies* (pp. 117–128). New York: Springer.

220 Duncan, T. G., & McKeachie, W. J. (2005). The making of the motivated strategies for learning questionnaire. *Educational Psychologist*, 40(2), 117–128.

221 Winne, P. H., & Jamieson-Noel, D. (2003). Self-regulating studying by objectives for learning: Students' reports compared to a model. *Contemporary Educational Psychology*, 28(3), 259–276.

222 Winne, P. H., & Perry, N. E. (2000). Measuring self-regulated learning. In M. Boekaerts, P. Pintrich, & M. Zeidner (Eds.). *Handbook of self-regulation* (pp. 531–566). San Diego, CA: Academic Press.

223 Greene, J. A., & Azevedo, R. (2010). Introduction: The measurement of learners' self-regulated cognitive and metacognitive processes while using computer-based learning environments. *Educational Psychologist*, 45(4), 203–209.

224 Bernacki, M. L., Nokes-Malach, T. J., & Aleven, V. (2013). Fine-grained assessment of motivation over long periods of learning with an intelligent tutoring system: Methodology, advantages, and preliminary results. In Roger Azevedo & Vincent Aleven (Eds.). *International handbook of metacognition and learning technologies* (pp. 629–644). New York: Springer.

225 Paquette, L., Biswas, G., Baker, R. S., Kinnebrew, J., & Segedy, J. (in press). Data mining methods for assessing self-regulated learning. In. D. H. Schunk & J. A. Greene (Eds.). *Handbook of self-regulation of learning and performance* (2nd Ed.). New York: Routledge.

226 Yeager, D. S., & Walton, G. M. (2011). Social-psychological interventions in education: They're not magic. *Review of Educational Research*, 81(2), 267–301.

227 Meece, J. L., Anderman, E. M., & Anderman, L. H. (2006). Classroom goal structures, student motivation, and academic achievement. *Annual Review of Psychology*, 57, 487–504.

228 Volet, S., Vauras, M., & Salonen, P. (2009). Self-and social regulation in learning contexts: An integrative perspective. *Educational Psychologist*, 44(4), 215–226.